MAGICAL MANAGEMENT IN THE CLASSROOM

MAGICAL MANAGEMENT IN THE CLASSROOM

Using Humor to Speak Their Language

Linda Marie Gilliam

ROWMAN & LITTLEFIELD
Lanham • Boulder • New York • London

Published by Rowman & Littlefield
A wholly owned subsidary of The Rowman & Littlefield Publishing Group, Inc.
4501 Forbes Boulevard, Suite 200, Lanham, Maryland 20706
www.rowman.com

6 Tinworth Street, London SE11 5AL, United Kingdom

British Library Cataloguing in Publication Information Available

Library of Congress Cataloging-in-Publication Data

Names: Gilliam, Linda Marie, author.
Title: Magical management in the classroom : using humor to speak their language / Linda Marie Gilliam.
Description: Lanham : Rowman & Littlefield Publishing Group, [2018] | Includes bibliographical references
Identifiers: LCCN 2017021329 (print) | LCCN 2017030519 (ebook) | ISBN 9781475832129 (Electronic) | ISBN 9781475832105 (cloth : alk. paper) | ISBN 9781475832112 (pbk. : alk. paper)
Subjects: LCSH: Classroom management. | Wit and humor in education.
Classification: LCC LB3013 (ebook) | LCC LB3013 .G543 2017 (print) | DDC 371.102/4--dc23
LC record available at https://lccn.loc.gov/2017021329

Printed in the United States of America

TABLE OF CONTENTS

ACKNOWLEDGMENTS

With this being my second book with Rowman & Littlefield, I want to first and foremost give a huge thanks to them, and especially *Tom Koerner*, for taking a chance on me! So many people I have encountered, and other teachers I know, have had such a difficult time trying to get their books published. I know from my own past what they are talking about.

Since I had never been published, and certainly was not a celebrity, the road to being accepted by a reputable publishing house was long and difficult. For some reason my manuscript proposal was passed along to the V. P. of the Education Department, and fortunately for me, Tom gave me a "thumbs-up" . . . after my agreeing to a few revisions! My first book, *Seven Steps to Help Boys Love School: Teaching to Their Passion for Less Frustration*, was under way.

However, then the hard work really began. Yet with the gentle guidance and expert editing of *Carlie Wall* at Rowman & Littlefield, my two books were carefully completed.

When it comes to humor, there are so many wonderful well-known comedians like Erma Bombeck or Phyllis Diller; both I grew up laughing with, for so many years. Their humor about everyday living and the funny situations we all go through made any difficult times a little less serious or stressful.

What a *gift* it is to have humor in your life. Even my amazing mom and dad, Needa and Harold Kreutz, made me giggle over the years! We *always* knew when "Daddy" was going to say something funny—his left eyebrow would raise up, his lip would curl, and with a twinkle in his eye, he would make a silly joke. I smile now just thinking about it, and it warms my heart.

Another person, *Wayne Sagar* of AAFO.com, and my life partner, attracted me fifteen years ago with his humor! We each make the other laugh, and bring out the best in each other. (Our two kitties, Angel and Muffin, often make us laugh with their interactions and strange behaviors! Aren't pets just the best for adding humor and joy to our lives?)

Lastly, my dearest friend *Terry Hendricks*, who is also a retired teacher and is now living in Hot Springs, has made me laugh the most, and for over forty years now! Her quick wit and positive energy is contagious, and people are drawn to her funny quips and warm humor. She taught high school for many years, all over the country and even in Hong Kong! I always envied her students, knowing how she could make learning about literature so much more fun, and easier for her classes to *retain the information* she taught humorously to them!

We need more teachers like Terry!

Most importantly, remember that:

> Some people make your laugh a little louder, your smile a little brighter and your life a little better. Try to be one of those people.

INTRODUCTION

Welcome to the wild, *unpredictable*, and crazy world of teaching and learning! Regardless of the need to constantly be flexible and ready for surprises, teaching can certainly be the *most rewarding* profession in the world. For it to be enjoyable and rewarding, however, a teacher has to know students' needs well and provide *great classroom management*, the latter being the key to everyone's survival.

Just by using a funny quote, the process can cause us to think a little harder at the meaning. (Hopefully, none of us can relate to the ones about how we aim to succeed in life or school, yet fail!) For instance, here is one by Ken Robinson: "For most of us the problem isn't that we aim too high and fail—it's just the opposite—we aim *too low and succeed*."

Beginning to organize your first day of school can be very daunting, and depending upon your comfort level, a little scary. Children often can be a real challenge if you do not "speak their language." What is meant by this will be explained throughout this book, entitled *Magical Management in the Classroom: Using Humor to Speak Their Language*.

Just knowing English or any other language is not enough by far. Children have such a different way of seeing relevance in learning, and often "tune out" the teacher, especially if they have *no ownership* of the material being presented to them.

Why is this? Well, children see the world in a refreshing and exciting way. Most of the time, chants, poems, songs, rhythms, music, and movement stimulate their brains to want to participate so much more than just a teacher talking to them or explaining skills. Try to remember the songs or fun chants that you once learned and *still know* from so many years ago. Those are still in your brain and usually bring a big smile to your face, right?

You might start to realize that adults and children think *totally differently* when it comes to humor. We, as teachers and parents, have to understand this before we can attempt to "speak their language."

Much of the understanding has to do with *how* the brain processes the information it receives, the *age* of the person hearing the joke, and the *background knowledge* that person has. For instance, the following passage, "A Senior's Travelogue," seems extremely funny to this author, yet to a child it would mean little and be very boring, due to their age and limited vocabulary.

A SENIOR'S TRAVELOGUE

I have been in many places, but I've never been in *Cahoots*. Apparently, you can't go there alone. You have to be in Cahoots with someone.

I've also never been in *Cognito*, but I hear no one recognizes you there.

I, however, have been in *Sane*. They don't have an airport; you have to be driven there. I have made several trips there, thanks to my children, friends, family, and work.

I would like to go to *Conclusions*, but you have to jump, and I'm not too much into physical activity anymore.

I have also been in *Doubt*. That is a sad place to go, and I try not to visit there too often. I've been in *Flexible*, but only when it was very important to stand firm.

Sometimes I'm in *Capable*, and I go there more often as I'm getting older.

One of my favorite places to be is in *Suspense*! It really gets the adrenaline flowing and pumps up the old heart! At my age, I need all the stimuli I can get!

I may have been in *Continent*, but I don't remember what country I was in. It's an age thing. They tell me it is very wet and damp there!

— Author Unknown

You can do your bit by remembering to show this funny passage to at least one other "crazy" *person who loves to laugh* . . . and has traveled this way.

In contrast, the following remarks from children show exactly how they think on a *totally different* level than we do. They make teaching so refreshing and *joyous*, helping us to realize how honest students can be, while taking everything you say "literally."

CHILDREN ARE SO QUICK!

1. *Teacher:* Why are you so late?
   Student: Class started before I got here.
2. *Teacher:* John, why are you doing your math multiplication on the floor?
   John: You told me to do it without using tables.
3. *Teacher:* Glenn, how do you spell "crocodile"?
   Glenn: K-R-O-K-O-D-I-A-L.
   Teacher: No, that's wrong!
   Glenn: Maybe it is wrong, but you asked me how I spell it.
4. *Teacher:* Donald, what is the chemical formula for water?
   Donald: H I J K L M N O.
   Teacher: What are you talking about?
   Donald: Yesterday you said it's H to O.
5. *Teacher:* Winnie, name one important thing we have today that we didn't have ten years ago.
   Winnie: Me!
6. *Teacher:* Glen, why do you always get so dirty?
   Glen: Well, I'm a lot closer to the ground than you are.
7. *Teacher:* Millie, give me a sentence starting with "I."
   Millie: I is . . .
   Teacher: No, Millie. . . . Always say, "I am."
   Millie: All right . . . I am the ninth letter of the alphabet.
8. *Teacher:* George Washington not only chopped down his father's cherry tree, but also admitted it. Now, Louie, do you know why his father didn't punish him?
   Louis: Because George still had the axe in his hand.

9. *Teacher:* Clyde, your composition on "My Dog" is exactly the
   same as your brother's. Did you copy his?
   Clyde: No, sir. It's the same dog.
10. *Teacher:* Harold, what do you call a person who keeps on talking
    when people are no longer interested?
    Harold: A TEACHER!

And finally, one for the *men* only:

11. "For Sale By Owner"
    Complete set of Encyclopedia Britannica, 45 volumes.
    Excellent condition, $200 or best offer. *No longer needed, got
    married, wife knows everything!*

Who cannot smile at some of those and realize how easily children
can make your day, with just the funny things they say! Some of those
jokes are so simplistic that an adult has to stop for a moment to even
"get them."

Actually, if we can go back to our own childhood, we can understand
this concept of early language development. Recall the silly songs,
poems, games, chants, or something as simple as hopscotch rhymes
from long ago and far away. Those are the fun memories of our youth,
and are *imprinted in our brain* forever. Many of them you can still
recall and repeat as if you learned them yesterday.

We as teachers and parents need not to be afraid to be a *little silly,
and even goofy*, when dealing with children, always remembering what
Tony Robbins said regarding being fearful, especially of appearing a
fool: "F.E.A.R. = *False Evidence Appearing Real.*"

All adults need to realize that our own "sophisticated language" can
often be quite boring, confusing, or even worse, unintelligible to little
children. How can we communicate with them, if we cannot try harder
to "speak their language"? In addition, how can we possibly teach them
anything that will be retained for very long? As teachers, we do not want
learning to be for "just that year" we are with them.

When observing children interact with each other, take the time to
really listen to what is being said. Do they speak the way you do? Are
their gestures like yours? Can you begin to see why a child can learn so
much quicker when paired with *another child* for learning games?

Don't we all discover, even after so many years pass by, we can still remember that "earliest genre" of language skills taught to us years before by others! Jump rope rhymes, silly songs, and chants are still very clear in our older brains. Why is that? Because we found them fun, silly, or *easily understood*. This is not to remind you of your age, or how old you might be now, but just to emphasize how adults and children "speak differently" when it comes to learning and communicating.

Let's open our minds to the following six chapters, and see if we can try a little harder to make our children enjoy learning, retain what they learn, and pass the joy on to others!

If we are truly caring educators or even parents, wanting our children to really hear what we are trying to teach them, we need to learn to speak their language!

I

WHO NEEDS HUMOR?

Laughter connects you with people. It's almost impossible to maintain any kind of distance or any sense of social hierarchy when you're just howling with laughter. Laughter is a force for democracy.

—John Cleese

A little nonsense now and then is relished by the wisest men.

—Roald Dahl

Humor is the key to life and enjoyment. We all feel more relaxed and comfortable when something makes us laugh, right? But when we think of who needs it more, it appears that children may benefit the most. Hopefully, this book will show you why and what you can do about it to help our children enjoy learning new and exciting things.

HOW IMPORTANT IS HUMOR TO ALL HUMAN BEINGS?

Extremely important! We have all seen that humor is undeniably infectious. The sound of "roaring laughter" is far *more contagious* than any cough, sniffle, or sneeze.[1] Laughing makes us feel very happy inside! When you make others laugh, it makes everyone happy. Laughter is a real "gift" to humans, but unfortunately is not used nearly enough.

Laughter makes you forget any problem for the moment, doesn't it? The feeling is like a total "body smile" or the best *natural drug* mankind can experience. When laughter is shared, it binds people together and increases happiness and intimacy.

THE SOUND OF LAUGHTER

A hearty, belly laugh means the same thing on every continent: joy.

But when we laugh with someone else, our chuckles may divulge more than we realize.

Scientists have found that people around the world can tell whether folks are friends or strangers by listening to them laughing together. And the ability transcends culture and language.

The study, published Monday in the *Proceedings of the National Academy of Sciences*, used a simple experiment. Psychologist Gregory Bryant recorded pairs of college students having conversations. Some were friends. Some hardly knew each other. He then isolated out just the parts in which the two people were laughing. Each cut was only about one second long.

Then Bryant and his colleagues at the University of California, Los Angeles, had volunteers listen to the clips of laughter and guess whether the people were friends or strangers. They ran the experiment in 24 societies around the globe, including indigenous tribes in New Guinea, tiny villages in Peru and cities in India and China.

People weren't perfect at the task. They were good at telling whether women were friends. But for other pairs—like two men laughing—it was harder. On average, listeners guessed correctly only about 60 percent of the time. That accuracy [is] slightly better than simply tossing a coin (which would give you a 50 percent accuracy).

But the results were consistent across all the societies studied. That's a big deal, says Robert Provine, a psychologist and neuroscience at the University of Maryland, Baltimore County, who wasn't involved with the study. "That suggest[s] we're dealing with a very basic aspect of human nature," he says.

For instance, a Hadza hunter-gatherer in Tanzania could tell two college girls in California were friends by listening to only one second of laughter.

"Laughter seems to be done by all people and all cultures," Provine says, "but details about what it means require cross-cultural studies. Such research is hard to do and is rarely done."

Neuroscientist Carolyn McGettigan at the Royal Holloway University of London agrees with Provine. "This study is really impressive," she says. "The scale of it is an achievement." But also, she says, it suggest that, even in the most remote places on Earth, a laugh among friends is a special sound.[2]

Studies have shown that laughter also triggers *healthy physical changes* in the body. Amazingly, humor and laughter strengthen your immune system, boost your energy, diminish pain, and protect you from the damaging effects of stress, which is more prevalent in our world than ever before.[3]

Best of all, this priceless medicine is fun, free, and easy to use for parents and teachers in their "Magical Management" style in the classroom or at home. Actually, the word "management" should be changed to "engagement!" The word "engagement" sounds less controlling and more enjoyable, doesn't it? We as teachers, parents, and children would love everyone "engaged" in what they are doing, rather than being "managed."

Laughter Is Strong Medicine for Your Mind and Body

Laughter is a powerful antidote to stress, pain, and conflict. Nothing works faster or is more dependable to bring your mind and body back into balance than a good laugh. *Humor lightens your burdens, inspires hopes, connects you to others, and keeps you grounded, focused, and alert.*[4]

If humor can do all these amazing things, why isn't it part of our curriculum?

With so much power to heal and renew, the ability to laugh easily and frequently is a tremendous resource for surmounting problems, enhancing your relationships, and supporting both physical and emotional health.[5]

Your sense of humor is one of the most powerful tools you have to make certain that your daily mood and emotional state is healthy. Support good health.

—Paul E. McGhee, PhD

After reading this powerful quote, we should all see how extremely valuable humor and laughter is to all of us and our well-being in general. In a way, we should be baffled that humor is used only now and then . . . when it sounds like a "Miracle Cure for What Ails Ya"!

Most teachers love their jobs fully, yet they learn how to look at life in a different way.

The following quote, by Heidi McDonald, is certainly true for most who teach:

> Sunday is a teacher's day of REST:
> the REST of the laundry,
> the REST of the housework,
> and grade the REST of the papers.

Laughter Is Extremely Good for Your Health Overall

Even children can poke fun at their own mistakes, and realize we all make mistakes . . . a very good thing for them to know and accept!

"I can't believe I just called my teacher 'Mom.' I'm so embarrassed!" —so many children have said!

By the way, according to Helpguide, *"laughter relaxes* the whole body. A good, hearty laugh relieves physical tension and stress, leaving your muscles relaxed for up to forty-five minutes after." Amazing!

- **Laughter boosts the immune system.** Laughter decreases stress hormones and increases immune cells and infection-fighting antibodies, thus improving your *resistance to disease.*[6]

Humor seems to be a "miracle drug," and it is FREE.

- **Laughter triggers the release of endorphins.** They are the body's natural feel-good chemicals. Endorphins promote an overall sense of well-being and can even temporarily *relieve pain.*[7]

Why wouldn't everyone want that?

- **Laughter protects the heart.** Laughter improves the function of blood vessels and *increases blood flow*, which can help protect you against a heart attack and other cardiovascular problems.[8]

Since heart attack is the leading cause of death, laughter is extremely important.

Learn the Many Benefits of Laughter

We as humans are very fortunate to have levity in our lives, but it is up to us to determine how much we want to experience. One would think that it would be the first choice to make our lives better. So, why do some have more in their lives than others? According to Helpguide.org, there are at least three major benefits to laughter.

The Three Major Benefits of Laughter:

Physical Health

1. Boosts immunity
2. Lowers stress hormones
3. Decreases pain
4. Relaxes your muscles
5. Prevents heart disease

Mental Health Benefits

1. Adds joy and zest to life
2. Eases anxiety and fear
3. Relieves stress
4. Improves mood
5. Enhances resilience

Social Benefits

1. Strengthens relationships
2. Attracts others to us
3. Enhances teamwork
4. Helps defuse conflict
5. Promotes group bonding[9]

After reading all the many benefits of laughter or humor, we can see a direct link to how important it is in creating the *best learning environment* possible! Naturally, teachers and parents only want the ideal environment for their children, and will go to many extremes to make that occur.

We as teachers must make that happen with a little more humor to *captivate our students*.

> I see the mind of the five-year-old as a volcano with two vents: destructiveness and creativeness.
>
> —Sylvia Ashton-Warner

However, when it comes to humor, some people can share it well, naturally being funny themselves, while others might want to learn how to incorporate it into their teaching and parenting; those need help in knowing how to do this. If you fit into any of these categories, this book will be an invaluable resource.

We cannot emphasize enough the importance of taking the time to learn new ways to engage your students. You will become that "fun teacher" they will learn and retain more from. By using humor, you will not only change your school year, but perhaps revamp your entire teaching career!

But also, remember the following quote that is certainly true of our children:

> Children are like wet cement. Whatever falls on them makes an impression.
>
> —Dr. Haim Ginott

So as teachers, which parents certainly are, try to always think about the impression that you might be leaving for youth to absorb.

Stay Emotionally Healthy with Humor and Laughter

Most of us will agree that in today's less-stable society there is a need for more emotional help than ever! And as Helpguide says, "Laughter makes you feel good. And the good feeling that you get when you laugh remains with you even after the laughter subsides. *Humor helps you keep a positive, optimistic outlook through difficult situations, disappointments, and loss.*"[10] We discuss this more thoroughly in chapter 4.

What Is the Important Link Between Laughter and Mental Health?

Helpguide says, *"Laughter dissolves distressing emotions. You cannot feel anxious, angry, or sad when you're laughing."*[11] What a great thing to have that can be used as a temporary diversion from those negative feelings! Mental health is such a huge part of everyone's life and especially of a healthy society.

One example of a person we know who always seems to know how to make us laugh is Oprah Winfrey. Here is one of her quotes about true friendship:

> Everyone wants to ride with you in the limo, but what you want is someone who will take the bus with you when the limo breaks down.
> —Oprah Winfrey

> **Laughter helps you relax and recharge.** It reduces stress and increases energy, enabling you to stay focused and accomplish more.[12]

Teachers, parents, and children need this more than ever before! In reality, we all do.

> **Humor shifts perspective.** This shift allows you to see situations in a more realistic, less threatening light. A humorous perspective creates psychological distance, which can help you *avoid feeling overwhelmed.*[13]

Many students really need this; we can all see "stressed-out students" from time to time who we can help tremendously with humor.

What Are the Social Benefits of Humor and Laughter?

> If the person you are talking to doesn't appear to be listening, be patient. It may simply be that he has a small piece of fluff in his ear.
> —A. A. Milne, *Pooh's Little Instruction Book*

> Humor and playful communication strengthen our relationships by triggering positive feelings and fostering emotional connection.

When we laugh with one another, a *positive bond* is created. This bond acts as a strong buffer against stress, disagreements, and disappointment.[14]

Laughing with others is more powerful than laughing alone, don't you agree? Many times, going to a "funny movie" is not nearly as funny when you go by yourself as it is when you go with someone else.

USING HUMOR IN THE CLASSROOM

When you use levity, laughter has the power to fuel engagement and help students learn.

The power of laughter cannot be ignored when we see that it can create a comfortable learning environment, *wake up children's brains*, and bring content to life.

Is Your Classroom Environment Comfortable?

> The expert at anything was once a beginner.
>
> —Helen Hayes

When teachers share a laugh or a smile with students, they help students feel more comfortable and open to learning. *Using humor brings enthusiasm, positive feelings, and optimism to the classroom.*

> Because I know that a good laugh eases tension, increases creativity . . . I will do almost anything to get the class rolling with laughter—voice inflections, exaggerated facial expressions and movements, hilarious personal stories (of which I have way too many), ridiculous examples . . . and I encourage my students to do the same.
>
> —Kaywin Cottle, Speech Communications teacher (NEA Facebook)[15]

> In my world, everyone's a pony and they all eat rainbows and *poop* butterflies!
>
> —Dr. Seuss

How humorous is that statement by Dr. Seuss, a man who could definitely relate to the way children love to learn! His descriptions are so visual and they make anyone smile just reading, and rereading, them. Teachers love reading books by Dr. Seuss as much as their students enjoy listening to them.

> In Health class, we learned the *cerebellum* is responsible for balance and coordination. When I trip over their backpacks, I might make a joke that my cerebellum is taking a nap.
> —Deirdre Sexton (NEA Facebook)[16]

"The key thing to remember is to do what's *comfortable for you*. Not only will it make you more approachable, it will also help put students more at ease in your classroom."[17] If a child is timid and shy, humor can be that "magical connection" you can make.

> The difference between try and triumph is a little *umph*.
> —Author Unknown

Naturally, many jokes are only appropriate for certain grade levels. The teacher must evaluate the age of their students and what is apropos for them. Again, like "beauty is in the eye of the beholder," humor is in the brain of the beholder! What is funny to one, to another is . . . dumb! (That even rhymes.)

> I like a teacher who gives you something to take home to think about *besides* homework.
> —Lily Tomlin

Here Are a Few Jokes for Different Ages

What do you call a friendly school? *Hi School!*

Why were the teacher's eyes crossed? *She couldn't control her pupils!*

Teachers always tell us to follow our dreams . . . *BUT, yet they don't let us sleep in class.*

Why did the teacher marry the custodian? *Because he swept her off her feet!*

What is the Great Depression? *When you get a bad grade in history.*

If the pilgrims came on the Mayflower, then what does the teacher
come on? *The scholar ships.*

Teacher: "Why were you late?" Student: "Sorry, teacher, I over-
slept." Teacher: "*You mean you need to sleep at home too?!*"

Stimulate Their Brains

As teachers or parents, we all dream of the time we see that "bright
light" in children's eyes . . . letting us know they are loving the learning
and engaging their brains! Teachers of the very beginning student can
peek into the future:

> If you really want to know about the future, don't ask a technologist,
> a scientist, a physicist. No! Don't ask somebody who's writing code.
> No, if you want to know what society's going to be like in twenty
> years, ask a *kindergarten teacher.*
>
> —Clifford Stoll

> During her research on learning and humor, educator-researcher
> Mary Kay Morrison looked at brain scans that showed high levels of
> activity in multiple areas of the brain when humor was used in con-
> versation and instruction.
>   "We're finding *humor actually lights up more of the brain* than
> many other functions in a classroom," says Morrison, author of *Using
> Humor to Maximize Learning.* "In other words, if you're listening
> just in a classroom, one small part of the brain lights up, but humor
> maximizes learning and strengthens memories."[18]

Teachers and parents should take the time to research humor; there is
an unbelievable abundance of materials at their fingertips for free!

Try to Bring Content to Life

> The best angle from which to approach any problem is the *try-angle.*
> —Author Unknown

Learning is so much more rewarding when a child can feel interested
and engaged in what is being taught. As stated often in this book,
people remember those teachers who could make learning fun and

even silly. Depending upon the age of the child, there are so many techniques available for teachers and even parents to emulate. Try to remember this:

> The best teacher of children, in brief, is one who is *essentially child-like*.
>
> —H. L. Mencken

Teachers can use humor to bring content to life . . . through games, parody, or comical voices (or wigs or hats). Students respond to their teacher's playfulness and appreciate the effort he or she puts into making a lesson fun. Here's how three teachers (on NEA Today Facebook) use humor to bring content to life:

> I make it a point to share my favorite silly books with the class. Then I ham it up as I read! They get fluency modeled for them and learn to love the books. It makes me more of a person to them, too!
>
> —Cherish Michael Blair[19]

Sometimes by putting in your name or a student's name, the characters take on new life and definitely make the readings more humorous! Of course, you need to get permission from the child to do this first. For some sensitive children, your action might embarrass them. Others will fight to be the "one" named in the book! As teachers and parents, we must always be cognizant of the sensitivity of different children.

> Whenever I can I use puns, anecdotes, or whatever humorous things I can think of to make lessons more fun, more relevant, and more effective. We laugh every day, and it makes being in school a little more fun.
>
> —Laurie[20]

Everyone has experienced funny situations in their life, or can remember an event that would also be humorous to others . . . why not share the memory with another? That sharing will make the students or child feel more relaxed, and realize at the same time that you can be approached more easily. Naturally, we do not want our children afraid to ask questions or try something new because they are *intimidated* by the teacher.

I teach French and Spanish. I have students practice vocabulary by trying to come up with funny combinations of words. Like *'helado de pescado'* fish—fish ice cream.

—Ann Braun[21]

What child wouldn't think this is funny, when picturing how "gross" fish ice cream would taste?

Teachers can just google a subject area like math, and find jokes for children about that. For instance, the following math joke could be used in the upper grades:

A math professor was administering the final exam to his students. He handed out all of the tests and went back to his desk to wait. Once the test was over the students all handed the tests back in. The professor noticed that one of the students had attached a $100 bill to his test with a note saying "A dollar per point." The next class period, the professor handed the tests back out. *This student got back his test and $62 change.* (This submission was by Olivia Armstrong.)[22]

You might find it hard to believe, but for any subject there is a joke! Just looking up jokes about cows came up with more than you would want to know! Here are a few:

Riding the train, a lady from the city and her traveling companion were riding the train through Vermont when she noticed some cows. "What a cute bunch of cows!" she remarked. "Not a bunch, herd," her friend replied. "Heard of what?" "Herd of cows." "Of course, I've heard of cows." "No, a cow herd." "What do I care what a cow heard? I have no secrets to keep from a cow!"

That joke may make many of us groan, but others may find it hysterical! The point is children will love you for trying to make them laugh.

Or you can try the question-and-answer type:

Q: What do you call a cow who works for a gardener? *A lawn moo-er.*

Q: Where do cows go for lunch? A: *The calf-eteria.*

Q: Where did the cows go last night? A: *"To the moooon" through udder space!*

SUMMARY

Every teacher's goal is to be *effective* in the classroom and help students learn. Educators want their students to be eager and engaged. Humor has the power to fuel that engagement. In addition to being more effective, the humor will help the teacher relax and have much more fun with their own lessons.[23]

This next quotes are better off to be shared with other teachers, not with the parents or children, for obvious reasons!

Summer: The time of the year when teachers can go to the bathroom when they need to.

—Heidi McDonald

The only reason I always try to meet and know the parents better is because it helps me to forgive their children!

—Louis Johannot

"Humor must be used in the classroom," says Pamela Matway, a sixth-grade social studies teacher at Sedgwick Middle School in West Hartford, Connecticut. "Joke, laugh, dance, sing, shout. I do it all; I think every teacher should. It helps kids stay focused on the lesson, and sometimes it even helps them remember ideas and motivates them. So, stand up on that desk and tap dance while you give instructions, talk in an English accent, or sing the answers to a homework assignment."[24]

Although this book will deal mostly with humor and its significance in teaching and learning, we do not want to forget there are many meaningful quotes for adults and children that are *not* in the humorous category. They may be about any subject, from weather to time.

Some of these quotes are for adults; others children can appreciate as well. Since we all need to not take ourselves too seriously, both groups can enjoy some of the following:

Weather forecast for tonight: dark.

—George Carlin

All right everyone, line up alphabetically according to your height.

—Casey Stengel

When you are courting a nice girl, an hour seems like a second. When you sit on a red-hot cinder . . . a second seems like an hour. That's relativity.

—Albert Einstein

If you enjoyed these, we can easily say, "but wait . . . there's more!"— just look in the appendix.

Education and Learning

When you have exhausted all possibilities, remember this: you haven't.

—Thomas Edison

Humor makes life so much more fun, yet many quotes about education do not need to be funny to make us think. Here are some thought-provoking statements and quotations that children and adults need to ponder:

- *Education and learning* are one of the most important ingredients to becoming all that you can be. How open you are to learning will help determine your path in life.
- *Education does not just happen at school.* It is not just about Math and other subjects. Your education and learning are happening all the time. They happen any time your mind is open to learning. We as teachers, parents, and para-professionals must take this opportunity to engage these children's minds that are so open and ready to learn.
- *Education is not just about learning facts, but more so about learning how to think.*
- *Education can be the most important influence in students' lives!* It is learning to make good choices. It is learning to act with purpose. We need more of our teachers, students and even parents to do this!
- *Becoming educated is a lifelong process.* It can be hard and frustrating at times, but it can also be incredibly exciting and enriching. Ask any teacher or parent that truly loves they're most endearing "job." They will tell you how passionate they feel about their role. [25]

You Know You're a Teacher When:

- You go to leave school at the end of the day and realize that you never had time to use the restroom ALL DAY!
- You get excited when you see "Back to School" supplies out in the stores.
- You can challenge young minds every day without losing your own.

—any teacher or parent!

Most importantly, learning and education can help you:

- Change the world
- Become a better person
- Reach your potential
- Eliminate your fears
- Make the most of mistakes
- Support your family[26]

Humor Is Useful and So Is Truth

Phyllis Diller was such an honest comedian, and she really hit the nail on the head with the following: "We spend the first years of a child's life getting them to walk and talk, and yet, when they get to school, *how to sit down and shut up!*"

In addition, this book wants you to know that when you feel drained for ideas, there are some inspiring quotations in this book's appendix that capture the power of education and what it can do for you and the world. You will also find lots of silly quotes, jokes, and knock-knock items you can easily use to entertain your students.

Even one of our well-known religious leaders, Joel Osteen, states: "Laugh a Little!"

In Osteen's *Today's Scripture*, he quotes from the Bible, and whether you are considered a religious person or not, this proverb has truth for all of us as humans:

A cheerful heart is good medicine, but a broken spirit saps a person's strength. (Proverbs 17:22, NLT)

Osteen goes on to say,

> God has given you a great prescription for living a long, healthy, and happy life: *Laugh, and laugh a lot!* The "medicine" of laughter is within everyone, but you may need to start taking it. Recent studies have shown that laughter boosts the body's immune system, reduces stress, reduces the risk of heart attack, and even acts as a natural tranquilizer. Those are health benefits everyone needs. That's why it's tragic to go through life with a stone face. The enemy has convinced too many into thinking that they need to be somber and serious in order to be a Christian. But don't fall for that trick. *God wants you to laugh and live well!*[27]

NOTES

1. https://womensconference.ce.byu.edu/sites/womensconference.ce.byu.edu/files/36c_0.pdf

2. Michaeleen Doucleef, "The Sound of Laughter Tells More than You Think!", Daily Life Credit PNAS (proceedings of the Nat'l Academy of Sciences.),1–18, April 11, 2016, retrieved December, 2016 from http://www.npr.org/sections/goatsandsoda/2016/04/11/473414068/ha-ha-ha-haha-the-sound-of-laughter-tells-more-than-you-think

3. Lawrence Robinson, Melinda Smith, MA, and Jeanne Segal, PhD, "Laughter is the Best Medicine," https://www.helpguide.org/articles/mental-health/laughter-is-the-best-medicine.htm

4. Paul E. McGhee, PhD, "Laughter Is Strong Medicine for Mind and Body," https://womensconference.ce.byu.edu/sites/womensconference.ce.byu.edu/files/36c_0.pdf.

5. Ibid.

6. HelpGuide, "Laughter is the Best Medicine: The Health Benefits of Humor and Laughter," https://www.helpguide.org/articles/mental-health/laughter-is-the-best-medicine.htm.

7. Ibid.

8. Ibid.

9. Ibid.

10. Ibid.

11. HelpGuide, "Laughter is the Best Medicine."

12. Ibid.

13. Ibid.

14. Ibid.

15. Robert McNeeley, "Using Humor in the Classroom, Laughter Has the Power to Fuel Engagement and Help Students Learn," NEA.org, http://www.nea.org/tools/52165.htm.

16. Ibid.

17. Ibid.

18. Ibid.

19. Ibid.

20. Ibid.

21. Ibid.

22. http://www.jokes4us.com/random/joke717.html

23. McNeely, "Using Humor in the Classroom."

24. Ibid.

25. Michael Stutman and Kevin Conklin, "Great Quotes for Kids About Education and Learning," http://www.inspiremykids.com/2013/great-quotes-and-stories-for-kids-about-the-value-of-learning-and-education/

26. Ibid.

27. Joel Osteen, "Laugh a Little!" *Today's Scripture* (Proverbs 17:22, NLT).

2

HOW HUMOR IN MANAGEMENT AND TEACHING AFFECTS THE BRAIN

Laughter is no enemy of learning.

—Walt Disney

Even our children's hero, Walt Disney, saw the importance of humor when it comes to laughter and learning. Defined by psychologists, a joke is an "incongruity that is recognized and resolved in some way."[1]

The following sections are adapted from Saga Briggs, "Intelligence and Humour: Are Smart People Funnier?"[2]

Did you know that whether you find something funny or not is based on your IQ? How funny to even think how much we care when it comes to our perceived intelligence! The truth is, once you do start analyzing the conceptual nature of humor, you quickly realize how similar it is to the way intelligence operates (through pattern recognition, but we'll get to that later).

INTELLIGENCE VERSUS HUMOR: SO ARE SMART PEOPLE FUNNIER?

There is a science-backed relationship between humor and intelligence. Understanding how the two are related could prove to be a key factor in understanding the human learning process.

Can We Predict Intelligence with Humor?

William Hauck and John Thomas, testing eighty elementary-level students, found a very high correlation between humor and intelligence (r = .91), but that was in 1972. What would we see today? Has humor evolved? Why or why not?

In 1990, biologist A. Michael Johnson published a study in *Perceptual and Motor Skills* that connected humor ability to problem-solving skills. Subjects rated thirty-two jokes for funniness and solved fourteen visually displayed mental rotation problems.

Subjects with faster mental rotation times tended to rate the jokes as funnier, which suggests that the right hemisphere of the brain—often associated with problem-solving ability—plays an important part in humor comprehension. Johnson's findings were consistent with previous studies of patients with right-brain lesions, who struggle to distinguish between punchlines and non sequiturs when selecting joke endings in a multiple-choice task.

In 1995, Holt examined the relationship between humor and giftedness in students. He suspected that intellectually gifted students would possess a more advanced sense of humor, noting that "many theories believe that the key concept of humor is understanding incongruity, and this involves a mental process like problem solving." The results confirmed his suspicions, as gifted students recognized and produced more jokes that relied on word play and resolving incongruity.

Around the same time, researchers from the Department of Psychology at Case Western Reserve University in Cleveland, Ohio, found differences in the comprehension, production, and appreciation of humor among students with learning disabilities.

In the study, twenty normally achieving second-graders and twenty-one fourth-graders were measured against fourteen fourth-graders with learning disabilities and twelve fourth-graders with developmental handicaps. Comprehension of humor was assessed by explanations of what made cartoons funny. Production was assessed by completion of cartoons without captions. Appreciation was evaluated by ratings of funniness and facial expressions.

The researchers found that children without handicaps comprehended the cartoons better than the students with intellectual handicaps.

Even More Proof Needed?

A 2008 paper published in the journal *Evolutionary Psychology* examined humor "as a mental fitness indicator."[3] Based on Geoffrey Miller's theory that intentional humor evolved as an indicator of intelligence, the researchers tested the relationships among rater-judged humor, general intelligence, and the Big Five personality traits in a sample of 185 college-age students.

They found that general intelligence positively predicted rater-judged humor, independent of the Big Five personality traits. Extraversion also predicted rater-judged humor, although to a lesser extent than general intelligence. "The current study lends support to the prediction that effective humor production acts as an honest indicator of intelligence in humans," the authors write.[4]

Also that year, Wierzbickia and Young tested three predictions about verbal humor: (a) intelligence is positively related to comprehension of humor; (b) difficulty of comprehension is positively related to appreciation; (c) intelligence and task difficulty interact in humor appreciation.

One hundred and sixty-five college students viewed cartoons and either rated captioned cartoons for funniness or selected one of four captions and rated the combination for funniness. IQ was found to be positively related to comprehension. In addition, students who recognized the jokes as complex appreciated them more, and students who struggled to process the jokes appreciated them less.

In 2012, Gil Greengross and Geoffrey Miller measured the intelligence of college students against that of stand-up comedians. Thirty-one comedians and four hundred college students were tested on humor production and verbal intelligence. Comedians scored higher than students not only on humor production, but also on verbal intelligence.[5]

Then Does Humor Predict Intelligence?

"Humor is not about comedy; it is about a fundamental cognitive function," says Alastair Clarke, author of *The Pattern Recognition Theory of Humor*.[6] Here's where the pattern recognition theme comes in.

Clarke defines humor in terms of pattern recognition—our ability to understand relationships and impose order on competing stimuli. "An ability to recognize patterns instantly and unconsciously has proved a fundamental weapon in the cognitive arsenal of human beings."[7]

Alastair Clarke explains: "The development of pattern recognition as displayed in humor could form the basis of humankind's instinctive linguistic ability. Syntax and grammar function in fundamental patterns for which a child has an innate facility. All that differs from one individual to the next is the content of those patterns in terms of vocabulary."[8]

Stanford researchers have even begun to understand specifically how humor activates different areas in a child's brain. Findings reported in the *Journal of Neuroscience* show that some of the same brain circuitry that responds to humor in adults already exists in six- to twelve-year-olds.[9]

In one study, children watched short video clips while their brains were scanned with functional MRI. In children, as with adults, the funny videos activated the brain's mesolimbic regions—the area that processes rewards. "(It is) in a less mature state than adults, but it is already present in children ages 6–12," says neuroscientist and child psychiatrist Dr. Allan Reiss, who led the study. "That's really interesting!"[10]

There was also high activity at the temporal-occipital-parietal junction, a brain region that processes incongruity or surprise. Reiss explains, "A lot of humor is, in fact, incongruity. Therefore, you expect something to happen and then suddenly there's a twist, something completely different happens and that's what makes many jokes really funny."[11]

The process of resolution requiring the integration of conflicting alternatives is a model of frontal lobe function, while the emotional payoff suggests an analogy with other phenomena (such as music) that link psychological expectancies with the brain mechanisms of reward.[12]

Reiss believes that humor helps make people resilient, improving their ability to cope with stressful circumstances.[13] "If you can interpret a difficult situation in a humorous way, as opposed to just 'this is a terrible fate befalling me,' that could make a significant difference in how your brain and body responds to the difficult situation," Reiss says.[14]

Recent research has shown that the stress hormone cortisol damages certain neurons in the brain and can negatively affect memory and learning ability in the elderly. Researchers at Loma Linda University have delved deeper into cortisol's relationship to memory and whether humor can help lessen the damage that cortisol can cause.

Gurinder Singh Bains showed a twenty-minute laugh-inducing funny video to a group of healthy elderly individuals and a group of elderly people with diabetes. The groups were then asked to complete a memory assessment that measured their learning, recall, and sight recognition. Their performance was compared to a control group of elderly people who also completed the memory assessment, but were not shown a funny video. Cortisol concentrations for both groups were also recorded at the beginning and end of the experiment.[15]

The research team found a significant decrease in cortisol concentrations among both groups who watched the video. Video watchers also showed greater improvement in all areas of the memory assessment when compared to controls, with the diabetic group seeing the most dramatic benefit in cortisol level changes and the healthy elderly seeing the most significant changes in memory test scores.

"Our research findings offer potential clinical and rehabilitative benefits that can be applied to wellness programs for the elderly," Dr. Bains says. "The cognitive components—learning ability and delayed recall—become more challenging as we age and are essential to older adults for an improved quality of life: mind, body, and spirit. Although older adults have age-related memory deficits, complimentary, enjoyable, and beneficial humor therapies need to be implemented for these individuals."[16]

Study coauthor and longtime psychoneuroimmunology (try saying that three times, and you might as well forget trying to spell that word!) humor researcher Dr. Lee Berk added, "It's simple: the less stress you have the better your memory. There are even changes in brain wave activity towards what's called the 'gamma wave band frequency,' which also amp up memory and recall. So, indeed, laughter is turning out to be not only a good medicine, but also a memory enhancer adding to our quality of life."[17]

Many scientists have wondered if there is a connection between humor and one's intelligence. Do not worry if you are never the funniest person in the room, however! The following information may encourage you to tell some of your worst jokes in a crowd!

End adaptation.

Maybe your eyes are glazing over about now with TMI (too much information) regarding our brains and humor? If so, we will take a "brain break" and give you a few jokes about the brain for a short time, so you can giggle a little.

We know neuroscientists are a fun group, so it didn't surprise us that there are many great jokes out there. Here are just three of my favorites:

1. What is a sleeping brain's favorite musical group (rock band)? REM.
2. What does a brain do when it sees a friend across the street? It gives a brain wave.
3. What do neurons use to talk to each other? A cellular phone.

SHOULD TEACHERS JUST STICK TO THEIR STUDIES?

After those three bad jokes, you are probably thinking just that. However, we as teachers or parents realize that if we try too hard to be funny there's a chance that we won't be taken seriously, which is a problem in humor studies generally. Sadly, there are some people who believe humor isn't a topic of science, and that it's a "subjective feeling" with nothing more to it.

We as educators must continue to be champions of education with meaningful quotes and humorous actions! Besides, they will, perhaps, make us appear even more intelligent. Plus, we as teachers must know for ourselves as well as our students that, in the words of George Clooney: "You never really learn much from hearing yourself talk."

Depending upon the age of the child, we see that what is "developmentally appropriate" for one child does not work for another. However, there is one thing that works with all children and that is HUMOR!

KINDERGARTENERS SAY THE "DARNDEST" THINGS!

Here are some darling things kindergarteners have said, and as you can see the humor reflects how that age takes what we say to them extremely literally! These should make you laugh out loud. [18]

A kindergarten pupil told his teacher he'd found a cat, but it was dead.

"How do you know that the cat was dead?" she asked her pupil.

"Because I pissed in its ear and it didn't move," answered the child.

"You did WHAT?!?" the teacher exclaimed in surprise.

"You know," explained the boy, "I leaned over and went 'Pssst!'—but it didn't move."

A small boy is sent to bed by his father. Five minutes later, he calls, "Da-ad."

"What?"

"I'm thirsty. Can you bring a drink of water?"

"No, you had your chance. Lights out."

Five minutes later: "Da-aaaad!"

"WHAT?"

"I'm THIRSTY. Can I have a drink of water?"

"I told you NO! If you ask again, I'll have to spank you!"

Five minutes later: "Daaaa-aaaad . . ."

"WHAT!"

"When you come in to spank me, can you bring a drink of water?"

An exasperated mother, whose son was always getting into mischief, finally asked him, "How do you expect to get into Heaven?" The boy thought and said, "Well, I'll run in and out, in and out and keep slamming the door until St. Peter says, 'For Heaven's sake, Dylan, come in or stay out!'"

A little boy was doing his math homework. He said to himself, "Two plus five, the son of a bitch is seven. Three plus six, the son of a bitch is nine . . ."

His mother heard what he was saying and asked, "What are you doing?"

The little boy answered, "I'm doing my math homework, Mom."

"This is how your teacher taught you to do it?" the mother asked.

"Yes," he answered.

Infuriated, the mother asked the teacher the next day, "What are you teaching my son in math?"

The teacher replied, "Right now, we are learning addition." The mother asked, "Are you teaching them to say two plus two, the son of a bitch is four?"

After the teacher stopped laughing, she said, "What I taught them was, two plus two, THE SUM OF WHICH, is four."

One day a first-grade teacher was reading the story of Chicken Little to her class. She came to the part of the story where Chicken Little tried to warn the farmer. She read, ". . . and so, Chicken Little went up to the farmer and said, 'The sky is falling, the sky is falling!'"

The teacher paused and asked, "Class, what do you think the farmer said?"

A little girl raised her hand and said, "He said: 'Holy Sh°t! A talking chicken!'"

The teacher was unable to teach for the next ten minutes.

A little girl asked her mother, "Can I go out and play with the boys?"

Her mother replied, "No, you can't play with boys, they're too rough."

The little girl thought for a few moments and asked, "If I can find a smooth one, can I play with him?"

From grades K–2, children seem to enjoy many of the same things. However, when they approach third grade, you might notice how their attitude, behavior, and interests change dramatically.

EXPLORING THE SECOND-GRADE BRAIN

According to Hank Pellissier,

> Your second grader will thrive best with a teacher who has high standards for her students. According to professor of psychiatry at UCLA School of Medicine Daniel Siegel teachers' expectations of students' abilities have a huge effect on student learning. In one study, teachers were mistakenly told that some of their students who had been previously identified as learning disabled were in fact gifted. After the teachers raised expectations, the students performed up to expectations. Children this age often develop affectionate relationships with their teacher; it's not uncommon for them to weep when the year ends. [19]

And a fun teacher who has made the effort to connect with each child by using humor during lessons will never be forgotten!

Goals Are Always Paramount

Dopamine levels are ascending in the second grader's brain. This neurotransmitter—which enables attention and motivation—increases its output when goals are attained. Your second grader will be ecstatically mind-enhanced if you help her carefully set, chart, and successfully reach her intellectual and physical ambitions. [20]

Our New Motto Is, "Read More for Success"

Reading fluency improves, aided by expansion of *Broca's area* and *Wernicke's area*, and the massive interconnection of neurons. Second graders might start reading because "they want to." [21]

By selecting books with humor, your child or student will want to read even more!

The following quote might bring a snicker to many who seem "addicted" to the new, and always changing, technology. Teachers and parents often feel so behind the times, when it comes to the understanding of newer programs on computers, cell phones, and games played on the TV . . . and many times they need to rely on their students or children to explain and show them what to do next!

So please, oh please, we beg, we pray, go throw your TV set away, and in its place, you can install, a lovely bookshelf on the wall.
—Roald Dahl (*Charlie and the Chocolate Factory*)

Cardio Cure = Brain Booster

Try scheduling at least 30 minutes a day for your second grader to run and play. They're ready for bicycling, and sports programs like soccer, swimming, hockey, and martial arts are outstanding brain-boosters. Old-fashioned school yard games—tag, double dutch and capture the flag—may be the very best exercise for young kids because they teach intense social and physical skills at the same time. Many seven year olds thrive with a physical challenge because their energetic, integrated sensory systems enable them to progress far quicker than adults in skills like skating and skiing. [22]

Better Brains = Better Food Intake

We all have heard the saying, "You are what you eat!" Sadly, too many of our children seem to want junk food before choosing a good, balanced meal. Now and then it is hard to avoid, but a constant diet of this type of "nutrition" can be very detrimental not only to the body, but to the growing brain, as well.

It is well known that your child needs a wide variety of nutrients for optimal brain growth. We all know this, yet in today's world it is difficult to control. Pellissier says, "Children need a wide variety of nutrients for optimal brain growth. Feed your child a balance of vegetables, fruit, whole grains, dairy, and meat, and limit their intake of candy, cookies, fruit juice, and sugary, salty junk food."[23]

Attention-Span Factors Matter

A second grader's attention span ranges from seven to 25 minutes; boys usually at the shorter end of the range than girls.[24] To encourage greater concentration capacity, encourage activities like meditation and board games—and limit TV. Studies indicate TV over-stimulates still-developing neurology, resulting in abbreviated attention.[25]

You Can Finally Increase the Humor Now!

By age 7, the Broca's area growth is larger in the right hemisphere. This beefs up language's emotional and prosodic components. Your child's comprehension is no longer limited to the "literal" which means that sarcasm and irony are within their grasp. The upside: They'll just chuckle instead of freak out when you mutter, "I'm gonna sell you to the pirates." The downside: They might start turning sarcasm back on you, with requisite eye-rolling: "Really nice tie, Dad."[26]

INSIDE THE THIRD GRADER'S BRAIN

The following sections are adapted from Hank Pellissier, "Inside the 3rd Grader's Brain."[27]

What can neuroscience teach you about your third-grader? Third graders tend to self-doubt themselves and overthink any response from their peers and parents. "Self-critical third-graders" are in a brain development stage known as learning "evaluation." Third graders enjoy catching parents and teachers making mistakes, but they'll also beg for praise to alleviate shame in their own perceived flaws. Why not turn some of this evaluation into humor? Let them know that "We all make mistakes; even the teacher!"

More High-level Thinking on the Horizon

Pellissier says that

> Third-grade brains' myelin-coated "white matter" now usually exceeds their nonmyelinated "grey matter." This means that their interconnecting brain has greatly strengthened the ability for high-level thinking, planning, problem solving, and information processing. You can help your child by guiding them towards "memory strategies," so your child can quickly file away the immense quantities of data that schooling requires. One great outcome of all this "white matter development" is that third-graders can be significantly less forgetful than second-graders.[28]

More Deep Reading Is Even Possible

Pellissier also says, "'Learning to read' is replaced by 'reading to learn.' This is a huge change for a child, a teacher, or even the parent. Parents can help by providing a rich language environment from the library."[29] They can also:

- Encourage reading out loud
- Quiz your child afterward on his or her reading
- Include your child in adult conversations with high-level vocabulary[30]

When you want more of a book for entertainment, a good one for most advanced second or third-graders is *Doctor De Soto* by William Steig.[31] Even older children can find this book very funny, since most of them have experienced going to the dentist.

This book is tells a clever, humorous story about a "mouse dentist" who treats mammals bigger than himself, wearing rubber boots to keep his feet dry when he's in their mouths. Steig's cartoony color illustrations make up the bulk of the book, and they are nothing short of weird and funny. The climax comes when a dapperly dressed but hungry fox comes for a new gold tooth, and the quick-witted dentist saves himself from ingestion by means of his professional skills.

Another book that boys find humorous is *Danny, the Champion of the World*, by Roald Dahl, illustrated by Quentin Blake.[32] Kids who loved the recent movie version of Roald Dahl's *Charlie and the Chocolate Factory* will surely agree that this edition of *Danny, the Champion of the World* is fabulous!

Danny is a boy who has a great life with his father. He thinks he knows everything there is to know about his dad, until one day Danny learns about his father's secret life as a poacher. If you want to know what a poacher does, and you want to laugh your way through Danny and his dad's dealings with a bad neighbor and pheasants, you must read this hilarious book.

Finally, let me introduce you to a book about a play on words—which children enjoy tremendously—that is also fun for the teacher to read out loud. Have the children guess what the mixed-up words mean. Since it has ninety-six pages, the reader can do a few pages a day to build interest. This type of reading keeps all children engaged in listening, identifying rhyming words, and learning vocabulary with spelling practice at the same time.

The delightful book we are referring to is *Runny Babbit: A Billy Sook*, by Shel Silverstein.[33] The "Nonsensical Wordplay" will entice readers to try reading this poetry aloud. A simple switch in the beginning letters of certain words makes language fun and the resulting sounds very funny. Just saying the title makes children and teachers giggle.

Your local library or school library are full of humorous books; just ask the librarian. Taking the time to find these special books for children will make your teaching more fun and very memorable for you and your students.

Time For More of "Me"!

The growing third-grader is developing a strong concept of "self." This can mean they're often focusing on their inner experience and outward appearance.

A third-grader will thrive best by running and playing at least thirty minutes a day. Most team sports are perfect for social interaction. Just keep an eye on them because they are very accident prone and hyperactive at this age. Tell them about times you felt like a "klutz" learning something new, bringing humor to their frustrations.

Third-Graders Need Kindness

Of course *all* children need kindness! However, now try to use encouragement and positive discipline to guide and protect your third-grader, instead of using punishment to make your child feel bad.

To support a third-grader's confidence and education, parents and other important adults should give loving, encouraging feedback. Minimize scolding and threats, and don't shout or spank for discipline. Maximize humor and levity, but at the same time, set boundaries and consequences for poor choices.

Our Classroom Mantra was "Hocus Pocus, You Can FOCUS!" Saying this to a student was a gentle reminder to stay on task. Isn't that better than an adult saying, "Are you daydreaming again, Dustin? You will never finish your work!" Children at this age can only manage to stay focused for eight to thirty minutes.

As we discovered, the changes in a child's brain just between second and third grades show us how complex the student's brain can be in learning new things. Although some of the information and research can make one's eyes begin to glaze over, it is important to understand the way children think, learn, and respond to new lessons.

So, now that we can see how much a child's brain can change by third grade, this fact will help us to see WHY the way we teach children is so important, both academically and emotionally. Fortunately, the one constant we can put into our "bag of tricks" is humor.

Everyone likes to smile or laugh at any age, but for children, the resulting comfort level makes them feel safe and more relaxed, and they can more easily relate to their teacher. Trust with an adult is established much quicker when humor is used, while making everyone feel more like a group at the same time.

End adaptation.

WHAT IS FUNNY TO ONE IS NOT FUNNY TO ANOTHER

Of course, we all know that what is funny to one age-group does not work for another age-group. The jokes or humor used must be appropriate to the age of a child. We may think something is funny as an adult, yet that same type of humor goes over a child's head. On the other hand, the silly things that children giggle or laugh about, we might think of as dumb or extremely corny. Why do kids think knock-knock jokes are funny? Probably because they are a play on words, and are short and easy to remember to tell someone else.

Therefore, as a teacher or parent, we should remember to find our own "inner child" to discover the types of things children find funny, and sometimes, even hilarious! Someone who passes gas or "farts" unexpectedly can have the class erupting into fits of laughter during a read-aloud story, or when a lesson is being taught. (Embarrassing as it is to say, this teacher finds it funny, too.)

Fortunately, the teacher can relieve the uncomfortable situation of the "fluffer" by first composing herself and saying, "Oh, big deal, somebody fluffed and we all do that, even teachers! It is a normal bodily function. When you are young or very old, it is hard to keep the gas from leaving your body. The smell is from what we have eaten, and you can always just say, 'Excuse me, please.'"

Then get back to what you were doing as calmly as possible. If they have trouble settling down, just change the venue, and start them doing jumping jacks! Who knows, maybe that will relieve all their gas built up after their lunchtime. Taco day, pizza day, or any day burritos are served it is almost a given that after-lunch stinky gas release will follow. Not great to share in an enclosed room, but just open a window. Why not try something active first, then settle down to a story?

Lisa Chesser wrote the following about different strategies or techniques using humor in classrooms.[34] Keep in mind that some would work perfectly in elementary schools; others would be too sophisticated. Save the latter for the middle school, high school, and college students.

During a recent class session, my students stared at me with blank expressions, glassy eyes, pasty and pale skin, and jowls drooping. I think I even saw a string of saliva hanging from the corner of one student's mouth.

I was reviewing plot structure. It was perfect except for the fact that I was boring them to death. So, I blurted out, "No wonder you like *The Walking Dead*, you look like zombies."

Suddenly, the students sporadically kicked and jumped and held their stomachs while laughing. Maybe it was because I was no longer talking about plot structure, maybe it was because I mentioned their favorite show, or maybe it was because they liked it that I finally connected with them.

We spent the rest of the class learning plot structure while laughing about episodes of *The Walking Dead*. Inside a classroom, the air thickens with time and words and problems and thoughts, lots of thoughts. Sometimes, there's a need to break the boredom.[35]

HUMOR CAN BE MAGICAL IN LEARNING

Humor in a virtual classroom enhances students' interest and participation, according to a study conducted by Ohio State University professors of psychology, Mark Shatz and Frank LoSchiavo.[36]

In the study presented at the American Psychological Society convention in Los Angeles, Mark Shatz and Frank LoSchiavo found that the use of levity in the virtual classroom can significantly boost student interest and participation.

There's no better way to gain the upper hand than with a twist in words, a lighthearted joke, or an outright laugh. The difficulty always lies in the delivery and the willingness of the teacher to seriously bomb. So, if you're willing, try out some surprisingly simple and often unique ways to bring laughter into your lessons.

Only one rule needs to be followed here. Never, ever use humor at the expense of a student's self-esteem. Joking with them is one thing. Putting them down is another. The classroom is not a comedy club. The use of comedy in the classroom is meant to engage students, draw their attention to your lesson, and offer inspiration.[37]

Since this chapter dealt with how a child develops physically, mentally, and emotionally, let's now move on to chapter 3, "Humor and Self-Esteem." You might be surprised how interrelated they truly are!

NOTES

1. Rod A. Martin, *The Psychology of Humor: An Integrative Approach* (Elsevier Academic Press, 2007).

2. Saga Briggs, "Intelligence and Humour: Are Smart People Funnier?" InformED an Open Colleges blog, February 21, 2015, http://www.open colleges.edu.au/informed/features/intelligence-humour-are-smart-people-funnier/. Used with permission.

3. Gil Greengross and Geoffrey Miller, "Humor Ability Reveals Intelligence, Predicts Mating Success, and Is Higher in Males," *Intelligence* 39 (2011): 188–92. https://www.psychology today.com/sites/default/files/attachments/95822/humor-predicts-mating-suc-cess.pdf.

4. Ibid.

5. Ibid.

6. Alastair Clarke, *The Pattern Recognition Theory of Humour* (Cumbria, UK: Pyrrhic House, 2008).

7. Ibid.

8. Ibid.

9. Erin Digitale, "Stanford/Packard Imaging Study Shows How Humor Activates Kids' Brain Region," January 31, 2012, https://med.stanford.edu/news/all-news/2012/01/stanfordpackard-imaging-study-shows-how-humor-activates-kids-brain-regions.html.

10. Ibid.

11. Ibid.

12. Ibid.

13. Ibid.

14. Eleanor Hayes, "The Science of Humour: Allan Reiss," *Science in School* 17 (June 12, 2010), http://www.scienceinschool.org/2010/issue17/allanreiss.

15. Federation of American Societies for Experimental Biology, "Fight Memory Loss with a Smile (or Chuckle)," April 27, 2014, https://www.sciencedaily.com/releases/2014/04/140427185149.htm.

16. Ibid.

17. Ibid.

18. From the minds, mouths and hearts of children, http://www.u.arizona.edu/~spikep/Humor/What%20children%20think&say%20items.htm

19. Hank Pellissier, "Inside the 2nd Grader's Brain: What Insights Can Neuroscience Offer Parents about the Mind of a Second Grader?," 2018, https://www.greatschools.org/gk/articles/second-grader-brain-development/.

20. Ibid.

21. Ibid.

22. Ibid.

23. Ibid.

24. See Linda Marie Gilliam, *The Seven Steps to Help Boys Love School: Teaching to their Passion for Less Frustration* (Rowman & Littlefield, 2015), for more information about this.

25. Ibid.

26. Ibid.

27. Hank Pellissier, "Inside the 3rd Grader's Brain: What Insights can Neuroscience Offer Parents about the Mind of a Third Grader?," 2018, https://www.greatschools.org/gk/articles/third-grader-brain-development/.

28. Ibid.

29. Ibid.

30. Ibid.

31. William Steig, *Doctor De Soto* (Square Fish, 2010)

32. Roald Dahl, *Danny, the Champion of the World*, illustrated by Quentin Blake (Puffin, 2007).

33. Shel Silverstein, *Runny Babbit: A Billy Sook* (HarperCollins, 2005).

34. Lisa Chesser, "Comedy in the Classroom: 50 Ways to Bring Laughter into Any Lesson," March 25, 2013, https://www.opencolleges.edu.au/informed/features/comedy-in-the-classroom-50-ways-to-bring-laughter-into-any-lesson/.

35. Ibid.

36. Ibid.

37. Ibid.

3

HOW DOES HUMOR HELP BUILD SELF-ESTEEM IN CHILDREN?

A person who has good thoughts cannot ever be ugly. You can have a wonky nose and a crooked mouth and a double chin and stick-out teeth, but if you have good thoughts they will shine out of your face like sunbeams and you will always look lovely.

—Roald Dahl

This third chapter can get a little serious and heavy, because we must first discuss the importance of self-esteem in children, as well as how important it is to all of us. Therefore, before we discuss the best use of humor with others, we need to have our readers understand that one's self-esteem, good or bad, will be paramount in how they live their lives.

The following sections are adapted from Nathaniel Branden, "What Self-Esteem Is and Is Not" and "Self-Esteem and How It Affects Virtually Every Aspect of Our Life". [1]

SO WHAT IS SELF-ESTEEM?

Let's now talk about all the important aspects of self-esteem, what it is and what it is not. In addition, we need to believe and know that *humor plays a specific role* when it comes to building self-esteem. Nathaniel Branden has some very insightful thoughts about self-esteem:

Four decades ago, when I began lecturing on self-esteem, the challenge was to persuade people that the subject was worthy of study. Almost no one was talking or writing about self-esteem in those days. Today, almost everyone seems to be talking about self-esteem, and the danger is that the idea may become trivialized. And yet, of all the judgments we pass in life, none is more important than the judgment we pass on ourselves.[2]

Having written on this theme in a series of books, Nathaniel Branden believes it is very important to discuss *what self-esteem is, what it depends upon, and what some of the most prevalent misconceptions* about it are.

CAN SELF-ESTEEM BE EXPERIENCED IN MANY WAYS?

Yes, states Branden! Self-esteem is a way of "experiencing the self." "It is a good deal more than a mere feeling," he stresses. "It involves *emotional, evaluative, and cognitive* components. It also has certain actions as in moving toward life rather than away from it." One must move toward consciousness rather than away from it, and at the same time look carefully at the facts. The individual must show self-responsibility.

Let's begin with a definition: "Self-esteem is the disposition to experience oneself as being competent to cope with the basic challenges of life and of being worthy of happiness. It is confidence in the efficacy of our mind, in our ability to think. By extension, it is confidence in our ability to learn, make appropriate choices and decisions, and respond effectively to change. It is also the experience that success, achievement, fulfillment—happiness—are right and natural for us. The survival-value of such confidence is obvious; so is the danger when it is missing."[3]

In addition, if it is not grounded in reality . . . and built over time through the appropriate operation of mind, it is *not* self-esteem. We have the choice to think or not to think. We control our consciousness. We are not rational—that is, reality-focused—automatically, states Branden.

Be who you are and say what you feel, because those who mind don't matter, and those who matter don't mind.

—Dr. Seuss

Building Self-Esteem with Branden's Six Pillars

In *The Six Pillars of Self-Esteem*, Branden examines the six practices that he has found to be the most valuable for the "nurturing and sustaining" of healthy self-esteem: *the practice of living consciously, of self-acceptance, of self-responsibility, of self-assertiveness, of living purposely and enjoying life . . . but most importantly, the practice of personal integrity!*

1. **The practice of "living consciously" is imperative!**

   You must examine the facts; being present to what you are doing while doing it. You also need to be receptive "to any information, knowledge, or feedback that relates to your interests, values, goals, and projects." We should try to understand not only the external world to self . . . but also our inner world, "so that we do not act out of self-blindness; purposefulness; and integrity." (*Try to see some humor in living consciously, in order not to take yourself too seriously!*)

2. **The practice of "self-acceptance" is difficult for most of us.**

   How many of us have the willingness to own, experience, and take responsibility for our own thoughts, feelings, and actions, without evasion, denial, or disowning? (*Using humor will make this so much easier to handle. Try pointing out and accepting your own mistakes!*)

3. **The practice of "self-responsibility" is so important!**

   Can you accept the actions and choices you make in life? Each one of us is responsible for our life and happiness, and for the accomplishment of our goals. Also, if we need the help of other people to meet our goals, we must offer values to them in exchange. Therefore, the question is not "Who's to blame?" but always "What needs to be done?" (*Lighten up whenever you can, become a "team player," and work as a team!*)

4. **The practice of "self-assertiveness" can be accomplished with very hard work.**

Can you always be authentic with others? Do you treat people with respect, without pretending to be who you are . . . or what you value? Do not concern ourselves with the disapproval from other people. Always be willing to stand up for yourselves and your ideas in appropriate ways. *Try to use a little levity* in dealing with others. (*A spoonful of sugar makes the medicine go down.*)

5. **The practice of "living purposefully" with goals.**

Can you identify your short-term and long-term goals, and the actions needed to achieve them by making an action plan? If so, try showing behavior towards those goals, and at the same time, monitor action to be sure you stay on track. Pay attention to outcome so you do not have to start all over! (*Smile when you make mistakes, but move on.*)

6. **The practice of "personal integrity" can follow you forever!**

Living with harmony between what we know, what we say, and what we do . . . might be the most difficult of all self-esteem pillars. However, by telling the truth, honoring our commitments, and exemplifying in action the values we say we admire, we can achieve personal integrity.[4]

Our Self-Esteem Must Be Earned

Some time when the kids are not seeming to want to sit still and learn, throw out the following: "There are three good reasons to be a student or a teacher—June, July, and August."

—Unknown teacher

(Children often think they are the only ones who cannot wait for the school year to be over. It is fun to let them know the feeling is often *mutual*.)

Branden emphasizes "that self-esteem cannot be attained by being showered with praise. Nor by sexual conquests. Nor by material acquisitions. Nor by the scholastic or career achievements of one's children. Nor by a hypnotist planting the thought that one is wonderful. Nor by allowing young people to believe they are better students than they really are and know more than they really know; faking reality is not a path to mental health or authentic self-assurance."[5]

However, just as people dream of *easy wealth,* they also desire high self-esteem, but without having to work hard. Unfortunately, with today's television, daily mail and especially technology, we soon discover these media are filled with those trying to "sell us this fantasy." We can even remember when "Spam" was something we ate!

> "So, if I bring a higher level of awareness to my self-esteem, I see that mine is the responsibility of nurturing it." No one, not our parents, nor our friends, nor our lover, nor our psychotherapist, nor our support group . . . can "give" us self-esteem. If and when we fully grasp this, that is an act of "waking up."[6]

> "In every job that must be done, there is an element of fun. You find the fun and 'SNAP,' the job's a game."
>
> —Mary Poppins

MORE BAD NEWS ABOUT SELF-ESTEEM

Apparently, when we do *not* understand the six pillars necessary for *healthy esteem,* we tend to seek self-esteem where it cannot be found.

Teachers who admit that self-esteem is important, without totally understanding what it is, may think that "self-esteem comes primarily from one's peers." Or they may believe, too, "Children should not be graded for mastery of a subject, because it may be hurtful to their self-esteem." Or "Self-esteem is best nurtured by selfless service to the community."[7]

The *misguided belief* that the measure of our personal worth is our *external achievements* is another misconception, Branden says. We certainly all admire achievements, in ourselves and in others. But this is *not* the same thing as saying that our achievements are the cause of our higher self-esteem.

His example: a depression of our economy might take away someone's job, but it cannot take away their resourcefulness, that will allow them sooner or later to find another one . . . or even go into business for themselves. Resourcefulness, or ingenuity is an action in *consciousness,* and it is here that self-esteem is generated. Remember, even in times of severe stress, humor can be a "godsend."

Instead of saying "Impossible," let's teach our students to say: "I'm Possible!"

—Heidi McDonald

Does low self-esteem cause violence?

Many agree that *low self-esteem* is an important cause of violence. Well, in reality, low self-esteem may have an influence in violence, but there are other factors at work. Today's violence appears to most likely be a result of "threatened egotism"—that is, highly favorable views of self that another person or situation *challenges*. Unstable or inflated beliefs in the "self's superiority" may be most likely to encounter threats, which leads to violence. The mediating process may involve directing anger outward as a way of avoiding a downward revision of the self-concept.[8]

To be completely realistic, none of us needs to be a "trained psychologist" to know that some people with low self-esteem strive to make up for their lacking by big boasting, annoying arrogance, and conceited behavior. This can be referred to as "compensatory defense mechanisms." Self-esteem is *not* manifested in the neurosis we call "narcissism" or in "megalomania."[9]

In order to think differently about self-esteem, "fresh thinking" might provide us with new ideas with important characteristics, hopefully allowing us to navigate *more humorously* and effectively through day-to-day reality. Think how much more enjoyable the day would be for everyone involved, when there is a giggle or two!

So, in conclusion, with one last observation, one of the researchers (Roy F. Baumeister), in an interview given to a journalist, explained his opposition to the goal of raising people's self-esteem by saying: "Ask yourself: If everybody were 50 percent more conceited, would the world be a better place?"[10]

The implication is clearly that self-esteem and conceit are the same thing, both undesirable!

Webster's defines conceit as "an exaggerated [therefore in defiance of facts] opinion of oneself and one's merits."

So, *no* . . . the world would not be a better place if everybody were 50 percent *more* conceited. But would the world be a better place if everybody had earned a 50 percent higher level of self-esteem, by living consciously, responsibly, and with integrity?

The answer is a resounding Yes!!! Our world would be a much better place, and what a pleasant world this would be! *Especially if humor could help to replace some of the negativity, bullying behavior, and depressing thoughts so many experience today.*

SO, WHAT AFFECTS OUR SELF-ESTEEM?

Self-esteem usually shows us our "perceived self-worth," as well as our ability to do things. Often this vision is *not* what we want to see, so it becomes our most carefully hidden secret from others.

Haven't we all seen people who sometimes try to brag about the wealth or prestige of their husband, the type of car they drive, the schools they attended, or the exclusiveness of their neighborhood? They have a need to feel more important than they are, which helps them cope. This is sad, but true and can be referred to as a "pseudo-self-esteem."

Whether or not we want to admit it, all of us know that the issue of our *self-esteem* is extremely important to us. To prove this, watch for the defensiveness with which "insecure people" may act when their errors or shortcomings are pointed out to them. This defensiveness can happen with adults or children.

Albert Einstein had it correct when he said:

Why is it that nobody understands me, yet everybody likes me?
—Albert Einstein

Other children may march to the beat of a different drummer, causing them to be alienated from a group who follows the trends. Always remind those "unique children" of the following:

Why fit in when you were born to stand out?
—Dr. Seuss

"If we refuse to betray our convictions, or persevere even when persevering is not easy, our self-esteem also rises. We may also notice that when we do the opposite, self-esteem falls. But of course, all such observations imply that we have chosen to be conscious."[11]

Hopefully, our children will be taught the importance of a healthy self-esteem and the power of living consciously, with *levity and self-responsibility*. They will be taught correctly what self-esteem is, why it is important, and what it depends on. If this truly happens, they will know that when they do not reach an expectation, *using a little humor* can always make the "medicine" go down more easily. By doing this, they will learn to carefully distinguish between *authentic self-esteem and pseudo-self-esteem.*

It is very important for the teacher to take the time to know each of her students extremely well. By doing this, the instructor or even parent can make a huge difference in how the child perceives him or herself. The goal for all of us should be to improve our perception of ourselves, by building a healthy self-esteem. Think how much more fulfilling our lives could become! Here is a darling quote from a lady who knows her "stuff":

> There are three things to remember when teaching: know your stuff; know whom you are stuffing; and then stuff them elegantly.
>
> —Lola May

Our children must be guided in how to acquire the knowledge of achieving positive self-esteem. If we can achieve this, they will have the ability to think, to learn and to respond with confidence to change. It is our *basic means of survival,* and cannot be pretended. The purpose of school must be to prepare young people for the challenges of adult life while *enjoying the journey at the same time.*

These same children will need these skills to be adaptive to an "information age" in which self-esteem is extremely important. As Branden points out, "In a fiercely competitive global economy, with every kind of change happening faster and faster, there is little need for unconsciousness, passivity, or self-doubt. In the language of business, low self-esteem and underdeveloped mindfulness puts one at a competitive disadvantage."

However, as parents and teachers, we cannot do our jobs properly, or communicate the importance of what we do, until we can understand the "intimate linkage" that exists between the six practices described above, self-esteem, and appropriate adaptation to reality. "The world of the future begins with this understanding."[12]

You may be thinking, self-esteem seems way more complicated than I really want it to be, and many of us agree with you. The formerly mentioned quote might be better if it read, "There are *four things* to remember when teaching: know your stuff; know whom you are stuffing; stuff them with humor; and stuff them elegantly." This author thinks Lola May could add humor or levity to their "stuffing."

HOW SELF-ESTEEM AFFECTS ALL ASPECTS OF OUR LIVES

Anyone who is familiar with the author of this book will not be surprised to learn that one of her favorite subjects is *self-esteem,* and how it affects virtually every aspect of children's lives. In *Seven Steps to Help Boys Love School: Teaching to Their Passion for Less Frustration*, there is an entire chapter dealing with the importance of self-esteem, especially in boys! Even when writing about something else, sooner or later self-esteem has a way of being discussed in relationship to learning . . . at home or in school.

"Self-esteem is the experience of being competent to cope with the fundamental challenges of life and of feeling worthy of happiness." The definition of self-esteem can be as important as it is controversial.

Nathaniel Branden points out that probably most of us have heard someone say, "But, I know I have accomplished so much so far in my life. *Why don't I feel prouder of myself?*" (Usually, these people are *not* thinking about business.) They might be thinking about their good grades in college, a very happy marriage, their now successful children, or their gorgeous home and cars. They may also believe that these "successes" should certainly lead to better self-esteem. But that is where they fail to "get it."

Naturally, there can be an assortment of reasons why someone may not enjoy his or her accomplishments in life. The better solution is to ask them "So, *who* chose your goals? You? Both pride and self-esteem cannot be attained by *someone else*, especially if it comes from a pushy parent who unfortunately "chose" your career for you!

Tying self-esteem to the approval of "significant others" and ignoring our own judgment in the process can lead to tragic consequence for our future.[13]

End adaptation

Why Not Love Yourself Just as You Are?

You are a unique human being, and there is *no one else just like you*. Why can't you love yourself just as you are? Most often there is nothing you *can* change, anyway, except your own acceptance of self. The way that people answer this question of "self-love" reveals a great deal about their childhood.

Children who are well-loved by their parents develop a sense of self-worth. This lasts a lifetime. Sadly, on the opposite side is that receiving "mixed messages" as a child can be devastating, and we know parents cannot have "do-overs" after years of this bad behavior. These *unfortunate messages* might include some of the following:

> I love you as long as you love me.
> I love you as long as you are being good.
> I love you as much as you deserve.
> I love you, but don't ask for too much or you'll be spoiled. [14]

One may remember such *mixed messages* from their childhood or not, but they all place conditions on how much parents love their children. *Conditioned love* is the norm, unfortunately, even though *unconditional love* is the ideal. Then, how can you change your inner image of how much you are loved and lovable? Deepak Chopra believes people can help themselves in positive ways. He says:

> The path to unconditional love involves two things. The first is finding the place inside you where unconditional love exists. The second is removing the obstacles that block you from remaining in this place. They two are connected, because you can't turn conditioned love into unconditional love by an act of transformation. It won't work. But the world's wisdom traditions speak of pure consciousness as containing bliss, joy, and ecstasy. It's by contacting this quality, known as Ananda in the Indian spiritual tradition, that you culture an appreciation of how to love yourself.
>
> Getting to the source of love isn't difficult. It can be achieved through meditation. Any contemplative technique, in fact, including Hatha Yoga, that centers you in a calm, peaceful place, will connect you with the source. Yet lightly touching this place doesn't keep you

there, because old memories, habits, and beliefs pull your attention back to somewhere else.

It takes time and patient [*sic*] to accomplish any transformation, and this is no exception. The first and most important step is to take an attitude of self-compassion, being as kind to yourself as you are to those you cherish in your life. Starting today, you can begin to follow some dos and don'ts.[15]

Why Must You Must Be Kind to Yourself?

In order to learn some new and better behaviors, let's look at some great suggestions from the *"do list"* of Deepak Chopra:

> Smile at your reflection in the mirror.
> Let others compliment you.
> Bask in other people's approval when it comes your way.
> Be gentle with yourself over small mistakes.
> Value who you are and stand up for yourself.
> Get to know yourself like a friend.
> Be easy on yourself about your personal quirks.
> Be as natural as possible, not worrying if you are pleasing or displeasing others.
> Speak your truth when you know you should.[16]

The *"do list"* is centered on accepting a *kinder attitude* for yourself.

The *"don't list"* is about *eliminating self-judgments*, because in the end, all of them lack loving yourself for who you are.

Why is Self-Judgement Detrimental?

Why do most of us have trouble accepting wonderful things said by others about ourselves? Is it because we do *not* believe what is said, or we may just feel embarrassed? Many then just try to brush off the compliment.

The following things on the "don't list" are ones we *should avoid at all costs*, unless there is a very good reason not to:

> Brush away compliments
> Reject other people's appreciation.
> Belittle yourself, even with self-deprecating humor.

Dwell on your faults as a topic of conversation.
Rationalize away the times when someone else hurts you.
Accept indifference from people who supposedly love you.
Associate with others who you can see have low self-esteem.
Silently swallow bad treatment when you know you should speak
    up.[17]

Chopra emphasizes that even "negative reflections" are useful . . . if you take them as *guides for change.* Obviously, the reflections of how you feel about yourself seem unending. Do you feel there are those who take advantage of you, or even take you for granted when they should not? On the other hand, maybe you allow that to happen? Wouldn't it make more sense to see this as how much *you* value yourself? Rather than trying to *change them,* change how you view yourself—in a more positive light!

This next "happy" list contains typical reflections in everyone's life, both positive and negative. Hopefully, you will have more of the positive! Why not print out the following "happy" checklist, and over the next week check off each time something on the list *happens to you*?

Does Your Sense of Self Show These Traits?

Positive Reflections:

Someone appreciated me.
I liked the person I saw in the mirror.
I received a sincere compliment.
I felt proud of something I did for myself.
I felt as if I belonged.
Someone expressed love for me in a meaningful way.
I felt lovable.
I felt well loved.
The beauty of the life I'm living really hit me.
I felt like a unique person; there's no one in the world quite like me.

Negative Reflections:

Someone criticized me to my face.
I frowned at myself in the mirror.

I felt guilty or embarrassed by something I remembered from long
  ago.
I put myself down while talking to someone else.
I felt unwanted, like an outsider.
I received what felt like an empty word or gesture of love.
I felt unlovable.
I sat through someone else's litany of complaints.
Something pointless about my life really hit me.
I felt bored by my existence and the people I keep seeing every
  day. [18]

Most of us could avoid these two lists, being too afraid of what might be
discovered as to how we feel about ourselves? Or, we might think that
noticing "negative reflections" is another sign of our own low self-esteem. Well, maybe it's not. Self-compassion is helped by being open-
minded and truthful with yourself, and daily. Remember, "practice
makes perfect," just like for your students!

Unconditional Love is the desired goal, and this only happens when
you move away from continual negative thoughts about yourself. Being
kind to yourself only occurs with your decision to change. Self-judg-
ment keeps us from loving who we are, just as we are.

Now let's move on to the next important part of our book, chapter 4,
to explore how humor can affect so many emotions that children and
adults share, like self-esteem. You might be surprised again, at how
much impact humor can have on a child when it comes to fear, sadness,
grief, intimidation, bullying, anger, and boredom.

NOTES

1. Nathaniel Branden, "What Self-Esteem Is and Is Not," http://
www.nathanielbranden.com/what-self-esteem-is-and-is-not; Nathaniel Branden, "Self-Esteem and How It Affects Virtually Every Aspect of Our Life,"
http://www.nathanielbranden.com/self-esteem-and-how-it-affects-virtually-
every-aspect-of-our-life.

2. Nathaniel Branden, *The Six Pillars of Self-Esteem: The Definitive Work
on Self-Esteem by the Leading Pioneer in the Field* (New York: Bantam Books,
1995).

3. Ibid.

4. Ibid.

5. Ibid.

6. Ibid.

7. Ibid.

8. Roy F. Baumeister, Joseph M. Boden, and Laura Smart, "Relation of Threatened Egotism to Violence and Aggression: The Dark Side of Self-Esteem," *Psychological Review* 103 (1): 5–33.

9. Nathaniel Branden, *The Art of Living Consciously: The Power of Awareness to Transform Everyday Life* (New York: Fireside Books, 1999).

10. Baumeister, Boden, and Smart, "Relation of Threatened Egotism to Violence and Aggression."

11. Ibid.

12. Ibid.

13. Nathaniel Branden, "Self-Esteem and How It Affects Virtually Every Aspect of Our Life," 2013, http://www.nathanielbranden.com/self-esteem-and-how-it-affects-virtually-every-aspect-of-our-life.

14. Deepak Chopra, "Do You Love Yourself Just As You Are?" *Huffington Post*, 2016, https://www.huffingtonpost.com/deepak-chopra/post_9635_b_7634756.html.

15. Ibid.

16. Ibid.

17. Ibid.

18. Ibid.

4

HOW DOES HUMOR HELP TO DEFUSE MANY PROBLEMS, LIKE FEAR, SADNESS, GRIEF, INTIMIDATION, BULLYING, ANGER, AND BOREDOM?

A mind is like a parachute. It doesn't work if it is not open.

—Frank Zappa

Zappa seems to know many of our minds. You could be wondering to yourself, *how could humor* even be considered in times of grief or any of the other serious problems listed in this chapter's title? However, as you might guess, fear, sadness, grief, intimidation, bullying, anger, and boredom are all very complex emotions within a child. And after learning all about the importance of self-esteem in our last chapter, we will find out that both humor and all those other emotions are very interrelated.

In the words of the Dalai Lama, "The systematic training of the mind, the *cultivation of happiness*, the genuine inner transformation by deliberately selecting and focusing on positive mental states and challenging negative mental states, is possible because of the structure and function of the brain. But the wiring of our brains is *not* static, not irrevocably fixed. *Our brains are also adaptable.*"[1]

The following section is adapted from Lynne Namka, Step Back and Breathe: Lesson Plans for Teaching Anger Management to Children.[2]

Childhood should be a time for free, spontaneous expression and for learning new skills to navigate the world. We now realize that good mental health is important for our children to succeed. Additionally, they must learn many skills that will allow them to develop friendships and loving relationships with others. By using appropriate humor, many problems children face can be made so much *easier* for them to handle as a child, and when they become adults, too.

They deserve *caring teachers and parents* who can help them learn the skills to deal with our constantly changing world. Children want to learn new, engaging and exciting ways to work with their strong emotions and conflicts. We observe that it is very difficult and challenging to be a child trying to "understand feelings" and how to succeed in today's world.

This author would stress that the most important skills missing in children today are *compassion, empathy, and compromise.* These are three emotions that could help children and *adults* get through life so much more successfully, not to mention helping our world become more peaceful. We suggest that teachers set up weekly lessons to address these important skills.

Role-playing is an excellent and impressive strategy for children to try.

> If you want others to be happy, practice compassion. If *you* want to be happy, practice compassion!
>
> —Tenzin Gyatso, 14th Dalai Lama

Emotional intelligence, according to psychologist Daniel Goleman, is the ability to understand and work with our emotions and those of others. It is found to be more important than intelligence or technical ability in creating success in the business world. [3]

Children can be taught "emotional intelligence" and skills to become more social in dealing with others. With this skill they can gain power over their emotions and make better behavior choices. All teachers and parents would love this to happen!

George Washington was wise with this saying: "It is better to offer *no* excuse than a bad one."

Of course, children have more self-confidence in handling stressful situations, when they have several alternative skills to draw from. *The appropriate use of humor is a tremendous tool in dealing with anger, fear, grief, sadness, and anxiety.*

We observe that early skills are mostly nonverbal. When you watch them, you see eye contact, facial expression, body language, and engaging others in social interaction. Social skills are reciprocal. Too much stress is placed on what we wear, the bike we ride, and the house we might live in. We need to let children know and believe the following:

> A *smile* is the prettiest thing you'll ever wear.
>
> —Author unknown

Little babies quickly learn to develop special eye contact, *smile responsively*, and look away to end contact *with the other person.* The "building blocks of development" naturally begin with the mother, but it might also be a single father. These early skills draw adults to the infant so that their needs can be met. They learn to "imitate adult actions" and begin playing with toys.

In order to understand and work with our own emotions, complex skill sets becomes a huge task of life for all of us. *Verbal skills* are learned along with other skills to communicate and play with peers. However, with so many bilingual children communication is more difficult. Since so of our children suffer from emotional and behavioral problems, going through life with these issues can be very upsetting to a child, their parents, and *even their teacher.*

Maybe writer Mary Ann Shaffer has it right when she said "I think you learn more if you're *laughing* at the same time." And tips for teachers and parents, schools, and communities on how to help children cope with loss, death, and grief are so necessary in today's unstable world!

It only makes sense that expressions of grief, and talking to children about death, must be geared to their *developmental level.* (Just like their learning in the classroom!) At all times we must be respectful of their cultural norms, and sensitive to their capacity to understand the specific situation they might be dealing with.

We know that children will be very aware of the reactions adults, who are important to them, might show by their discussions and actions. The emotional child will need time to discus and react to information about death and tragedy. In fact, for primary-grade children, how adults react to the situation plays an important role in how the child can handle their situation successfully.

End adaptation.

Reactions Children Might Display with the Death of Significant Others

The National Association of School Psychologists, "Helping Children Cope with Loss, Death, and Grief Tips for Teachers and Parents," has information that guides us through the grief of a child. All teachers will encounter one of these desperate children during their career, so it is imperative to know these tips *ahead of time. By doing this first, everyone will benefit!*

Here are some behaviors to watch for:

- *Emotional shock and at times an apparent lack of feelings*. This serves to help the child detach from the pain of the moment, and they seem to be in denial at times;
- *Regressive or immature behaviors, such as needing to be rocked or held*. The child has difficulty separating from parents or significant others. They might need to sleep in parent's bed. Child shows apparent difficulty completing tasks that are well within the child's ability level;
- *Explosive emotions or acting-out behaviors*. This shows the child's "internal feelings" of anger, terror, frustration, and helplessness. Acting out may reflect their true insecurity. This might be a way to seek control over a situation over which they have little or no control;
- *Asking the same questions over and over.* It is not because they do not understand the facts, but rather because the information is so hard to believe or accept. Repeated questions might help the listeners anyway, so allow them to ask away. The questions could determine if the child is responding to misinformation, or the real trauma of the event.[4]

How Can We Help Children Cope Better?

Dr. Alan Wolfelt, Director of the Center for Loss and Life Transition in Fort Collins, Colorado, shares the following tips to help teachers, parents, and other caregivers. Hopefully they can help support children who have experienced the loss of parents, friends, or loved ones. Some of these helpful recommendations are:

1. **Allow children to be the teachers about their grief experiences:** Adults must give children the opportunity to "tell their story." Show them you are a good listener and really care about their stress. Make sure they meet immediately with the school psychologist!

2. **Don't assume that every child in a certain age-group understands death in the same way or with the same feelings:** All children are different, and their view of the world has been shaped by unique experiences. Parents and teachers must take all of this into consideration when dealing with the subject of death.

3. **Grieving is a process, not an event:** Teachers, parents, and schools need to allow enough time for each child to grieve in the manner that works for that child. Putting pressure on children to resume "normal" activities can cause additional problems. The child needs time to deal with their emotional pain, which may take longer than you expect.

4. **Don't lie or tell half-truths to children about the tragic event:** Children are very insightful about honesty with adults. They will see through false information, and wonder why you do not trust them with the truth. Lies do not help the child through the healing process or help develop effective coping strategies. They need skills for life's future tragedies or losses. Children are often brighter and more sensitive than we give them credit for.

5. **Help all children, regardless of age, to understand loss and death:** The child must be allowed to guide adults as to the need for more information. Often clarification of the information presented to them is needed. Give the child information at the level that they can understand . . . sadly, loss and death are both part of the "cycle of life" that children need to understand. Discuss how the loss of pets is also a part of that cycle.

6. **Encourage children to ask questions about loss and death:** Teachers and parents need to be less anxious about *not* knowing all the answers. Sometimes the child just needs a caring listener,

not someone to solve their loss. Always treat their questions with respect. Be willing to help the child find his or her own answers.

7. **Don't assume that children always grieve in an orderly or predictable way:** We all grieve in different ways, right? There is no one right way for people to move through the grieving process. This grieving may last for months and even years!

8. **Let children know that you really want to understand what they are feeling, or what they need:** Sometimes children are upset but they can't tell you what will be helpful. How would they know? Only those who have gone through a similar tragedy can help or give suggestions. The children certainly need the time and encouragement to share their feelings with you. By doing this you may enable them to sort out their feelings in a healthier way.

9. **Children will need long-lasting support:** Naturally, the more losses the child or adolescent suffers, the more difficult it will be to recover. Try to develop multiple supports for children who suffer significant losses. This is especially true if they have lost a parent who was their major source of support. Now their life has changed forever!

10. **Keep in mind that grief work is hard:** It is hard work for teachers and parents, but harder for children. Time is not of the essence, and we all need to be patient. Give the child the time needed to work through this most difficult, emotional situation.

11. **Be aware of your own need to grieve:** It only makes sense that adults who have lost a loved one will be far more able to help children work through their grief. This will only happen, however, if they get help themselves. They might have to focus on the children in their care, but not at the expense of their own emotional needs. For some families, it may be important to seek family grief counseling, as well as individual sources of support. School counseling can be a starting point.[5]

Great Resources to Help You Identify Symptoms of Severe Stress and Grief Reactions

It is important for all of us to remember that the children who are physically and emotionally closest to an "event of tragedy," may very well experience the most dramatic feelings of fear, anxiety, and loss. In our changed society, anything can happen, and has!

They may have personally lost a loved one, or know of friends and schoolmates who have been devastated by the tragedy. Teachers and parents need to carefully observe these children for *signs of traumatic stress, depression, or even suicidal thinking*, and seek the help of the school's psychologist or even secure professional help when necessary. Many valuable resources are available at the National Association of School Psychologists website—www.nasponline.org.

For Caregivers

- Deaton, R. L., and W. A. Berkan. (1995). *Planning and Managing Death Issues in the Schools: A Handbook.* Westport, CT: Greenwood Publishing Group.
- Mister Rogers Website: www.misterrogers.org (see booklet on Grieving for children 4–10 years)
- Webb, N. B. (1993). *Helping Bereaved Children: A Handbook for Practitioners.* New York: Guilford Press.
- Wolfelt, A. (1983). *Helping Children Cope with Grief.* Bristol, PA: Accelerated Development.
- Wolfelt, A. (1997). *Healing the Bereaved Child: Grief Gardening, Growth through Grief and Other Touchstones for Caregivers.* Ft. Collins, CO: Companion.
- Worden, J. W. (1996). *Children and Grief: When a Parent Dies.* New York: Guilford Press

For Children

- Gootman, M. E. (1994). *When a Friend Dies: A Book for Teens about Grieving and Healing.* Minneapolis: Free Spirit Publishing.
- Greenlee, S. (1992). *When Someone Dies.* Atlanta: Peachtree Publishing. (Ages 9–12).
- Helping Children Cope with Death, The Dougy Center for Grieving Children, www.dougy.org.
- Wolfelt, A. (2001). *Healing your Grieving Heart for Kids.* Ft. Collins, CO: Companion. (See also similar titles for teens and adults).[6]

HABITUALLY ANGRY CHILDREN USUALLY SUFFER FROM SKILL DEFICITS

A little *nonsense* now and then is relished by the wisest men.

—Roald Dahl

The following sections are adapted from Lynne Namka, Step Back and Breathe: Lesson Plans for Teaching Anger Management to Children.[7]

Lynne Namka explains that angry children often do not interpret social situations correctly and respond with unwanted *aggressive behavior.* Subsequently, they now believe that getting back at someone must be done. Angry children may even believe that retaliation or "self-righteous expression" of anger is normal behavior. They usually blame others for their problems, and refuse to take responsibility for their own actions. They will not allow themselves to see that they are at fault for some of their problems. The angry child who acts out often ends up with peer rejection and isolation in the class.

Unfortunately, angry children and adults have missed learning some of the *basic skills* in handling conflict and getting along with others. They have probably *not* been able to have much silliness or "nonsense" growing up. This nonsense might have helped them to ease some stressful times. Could humor have changed things? We say, "Yes!"

Habitually angry children have not learned compassion or empathy. They do not see things from other people's point of view. Without the abilities to deal with frustration after losing a game, or not getting something they want, they act out in anger.

In other words, they have not learned the skill of "consequential thinking" or having empathy for others. They do not know how to rationalize their thinking and cannot stop making judgments about certain people.

Habitual, Hostile Expression of Anger Perpetuates an Environment That Is Unhealthy

Some angry children sadly "keep negative things" inside and are *secretly angry*. They are not comfortable in letting others know how they feel. They rarely talk about or express their anger directly to others. They almost seem to be ticking time bombs and who knows how they will grow up and deal with stress?

The angry child who vents may feel better for a short time but underneath he often feels worse for "losing his cool." Or he may hold on to his anger, rationalizing it to himself and others that it is his right to behave in violent ways. Unfortunately, children from dysfunctional families do not have positive skills modeled for them. They grow up possibly learning to use manipulation, addictive behavior, and violence when coping with stress.

Other children do not learn skills of social interaction naturally due to some neurological impairment. The rigidity of thinking associated with neurological impairment causes the child to become locked into negative coping patterns of dealing with stressful situations that bring him more stress.

End adaptation.

THE SOCIAL POWER OF HUMOR

> I agree with your Facebook post, but I won't "LIKE" it, because it has too many grammatical errors.
> —Heidi McDonald

Embarrassment can be one of our worst fears, but how about trying this?

> We all enjoy the obvious humor in certain situations, and sometimes it is from our *own embarrassing* ones. Why not share them?
> —Linda Marie Gilliam

According to Helpguide, humor can help you:

- **Form a stronger bond with other people**. We see how laughter binds people together. Remember that your health and happiness depend, to a large degree, on the quality of your relationships with people close to you.
- **Smooth over your differences**. What a wonderful way to smooth over our differences, whether they are real or just per-

ceived. Try using gentle humor to help you address even the most sensitive issues, such as money, race, sex, or even in-laws!

- **Defuse tension in the room**. When you notice things getting a little "uptight," a well-timed joke can ease a tense situation and help you resolve disagreements before they get even worse. Use the joke as a "spoonful of sugar" to help the "medicine go down."
- **Overcome problems and setbacks that come along**. Humor can help you with all frustrations. A sense of humor is the key to your resilience. You will discover that a sense of humor helps you take many hardships in stride, and even bounce back from adversity and loss. You will feel better in the process, if you give levity a chance!
- **Try to always put things into perspective**. Humor can help you defuse a problem that might otherwise seem overwhelming and damage a relationship. If we analyze the problem, most situations are not as horrible as they appear. Try to look at your roadblock from a playful and humorous point of view
- **Being more creative is so important**. Humor and playfulness can loosen you up, energize your thinking, and inspire creative problem-solving for any relationship issue.[8]

Using Humor to Manage and Defuse Conflict Is Very Valuable

I am *not* a superhero. I am something more powerful: I AM A TEACHER! I don't need a cape because I'm lifted up by the *amazing and inspiring students* that I teach!

—Author unknown

Remember, Helpguide continues, that "*how* you manage conflict can often determine how successful your relationships will be."[9] We find that conflict is an inevitable part of all relationships. Conflict may become a disagreement between two people, or simply annoyances that have built up over time.

If we are human, this situation of conflict will happen sometimes in our lives.

When conflict and disagreement appear in your relationship with a student, parent, or coworker, *humor and playfulness can help lighten things up* and help us to reconnect. This conflict can be "perceived real" by a student, parent, or even another teacher you work with. Whether it is real to you or not, the situation needs to be alleviated soon.

Used skillfully and respectfully, "a little lighthearted humor can quickly turn conflict and tension into an opportunity for shared fun and intimacy. It allows you to get your point across without getting the other person's defenses up . . . or hurting his or her feelings."[10]

Use Funny Knock-Knock Jokes for Kids

Why do children giggle when the "class clown" does or says something that seems stupid to us? It is because the students all "get it," it tickles their funny bone, although it seems so dumb to teachers or parents.

Why do knock-knock jokes immediately wake up your children and make them want to participate . . . and even make up their own to try out on others? Probably all of us have several right now we could recite.

Try some of these in your own class or in the home and see how the children all pay attention, even your hardest-to-engage students. Use the jokes for a smoother transition into a new skill area being taught, or just to regroup your class for total involvement!

> Discover *wildlife* . . . become a teacher!
>
> —Author unknown

The website jokes4us.com has hundreds of simple, silly, and short knock-knock jokes for many categories.[11] Naturally, choose the ones appropriate for your age-group.

For example:

Knock, knock.

Who's there?

Pecan

Pecan who?

Pecan on someone your own size!

Yes . . . again, this may seem extremely dumb to us, but children love it, and you can easily open a discussion with students about bullying and how to show kindness, instead, toward their classmates. Naturally, with regard to this knock-knock joke you also explain to them that size has nothing to do with it, since picking on others is cruel and unusual punishment.

Teachers soon find, often to their chagrin, that the quote "the sillier the better" fits most children in their classroom. And if we want to establish a trust and rapport with our students, with better communication, we must try harder to "SPEAK THEIR LANGUAGE"!

Who knows, by doing this teachers might even discover their own "inner child," and see that they, too, can have more fun while teaching! *Humor is contagious*, just like your enthusiasm demonstrated in teaching.

Here is another knock-knock joke to make you groan, but it will also get your students listening, smiling, and learning at the same time. Write this one on the board while starting a new math lesson:

Knock, knock.

Who's there?

Two 4s

Two 4s who?

No need to go to lunch . . . *we already have 8!*

(Make sure you let them know that with jokes we can use *improper* grammar!)

Next ask, "Who could come up to the board and write the real number equation for this?" Watch the hands shoot into the air, wanting to be the one to get to write on the board. (4 + 4 = 8) You might have them draw simple objects as well to further help those "visual learners": 4 apples + 4 bananas = 8 apples and bananas. (Remember to always be as creative as you can!)

> "*Creativity:* Take the obvious, add a cupful of brains, a generous pinch of imagination, a bucketful of courage and daring, stir well and bring to a boil."
>
> —Bernard Baruch

Try to be honest, now—isn't this a better way to start off a new math lesson than saying, "Please open your math books to page 10"? When you approach teaching this boring adult way, you have already lost many of your struggling students, or even those not particularly fond of math!

Many instructors *need more humor* . . . allowed in correcting tests, and whether the answer is correct or not, some credit should be given for "creative answers." A few of these might be over the top . . . but you must agree, some can make all of us smile or even laugh out loud?

Even older children must be entitled to show humor and creativity on tests! We all have had times when we did not study for a test, or as an adult were not prepared for a presentation or interview, due to an unexpected interruption of life, right? So why shouldn't students be allowed some slack as well? How do you feel when you read the random answers given on a variety of tests? This exercise, based on a commonly told social media tale, might tell you, if as a teacher, you have some work to do in the area of "lightening up" in your classroom!

STUDENT WHO OBTAINED 0 PERCENT ON VARIED EXAM

This author and teacher might have given him 100 percent! Each answer is absolutely grammatically correct, and funny too. The *teacher who graded the student* had no sense of humor, unfortunately. Of course, we want our children to learn and do well on the tests we give them, but we should never stifle their levity, and maybe this student should get "extra credit" for thinking outside the box, while entertaining his or her teacher as well.

Q1. In which battle did Napoleon die?
his last battle
Q2. Where was the Declaration of Independence signed?
at the bottom of the page
Q3. River Ravi flows in which state?
liquid
Q4. What is the main reason for divorce?
marriage
Q5. What is the main reason for failure?
exams

Q6. What can you never eat for breakfast?
Lunch & dinner
Q7. What looks like half an apple?
The other half
Q8. If you throw a red stone into the blue sea what it will become?
Wet
Q9. How can a man go eight days without sleeping?
No problem, he sleeps at night.
Q10. How can you lift an elephant with one hand?
You will never find an elephant that has one hand.
Q11. If you had three apples and four oranges in one hand and four
    apples and three oranges in other hand, what would you have?
Very large hands
Q12. If it took eight men ten hours to build a wall, how long would it
    take four men to build it?
No time at all, the wall is already built.
Q13. How can you drop a raw egg onto a concrete floor without
    cracking it?
Any way you want, concrete floors are very hard to crack.

—Author unknown

SPREAD SOME LAUGHTER, SHARE THE CHEER. LET'S BE HAPPY, WHILE WE'RE HERE!

Knock-knock jokes seem to *make adults groan*, but this simple format is adored by children. Not all of these jokes are tremendously amusing to us, but many will make children giggle and love you for telling a joke before starting a new lesson—such an easy way to win over good listeners! This telling of riddles and jokes can help so many angry, bullied, sad, stressed, abused, intimidated, fearful, even bored children. And as stated earlier, the bond of trust is further established.

Football players have the Super Bowl.
Runners have the Olympics.
Teachers Have "Back To School."
Armed with new ideas, fresh views,
a stapler, and glue. GAME ON!

—Author unknown

Defusing many of these problems is not always easy, but humor can certainly help change those negative feelings for the time being. We think humor is a "magical management tool." Anyone can learn to use humor in the home or in the classroom. Many of the children we work with have so many unfortunate scenarios in their lives that are sometimes unknown to all. If nothing more than a pleasant distraction, *humor can destress many of these children*!

Students will love you for helping them experience a giggle or laugh, which they may rarely have in their homes. In a way, levity is a "gift" you are giving to them to see humor associated with a learning environment.

He who laughs most, learns best.

—John Cleese

Grown-ups have trouble seeing the humor in silly jokes, and especially ones like the following:

Knock, knock.

Who's there?

Canoe!

Canoe who?

Canoe come out and play with me today?

Knock, knock.

Who's there?

Who!

Who who?

That's what an owl says!

Knock, knock.

Who's there?

Lettuce. Lettuce who?

Lettuce in, it's cold out here.

You may feel that most knock-knock jokes have very little appeal, but children see them totally differently and enjoy their humor. In addition to being funny, they are short and easy for a child to remember and tell. Let them share their special ones with you, and giggle no matter what! You might even create or find some of your own to share with them?

We cannot leave out those children who are not wild about dinosaurs, and maybe prefer *jokes about animals* in general. Here a few you can use to get their attention when beginning a new lesson. Even better, write one on the board as they read the question; then ask who knows the answer. All children like to give their own guess, and it piques the interest of the entire class.

Q: Why don't they play poker in the jungle?
    A: *Too many cheetahs.*
    Q: What is the difference between a cat and a comma?
    A: *One has the paws before the claws and the other has the clause before the pause.*
    Q: Where do dogs go when they lose their tails?
    A: *To the retail store.*[12]

You might be saying that your eyes are starting to glaze over from *"dino sore eye us"* . . . yes, this one is very bad, but many silly students will think that even this is sort of funny!

Well, there are plenty of jokes for a few lessons shared, but there are many other ways to involve humor in your teaching. Jokes are just very quick to do and easy to remember, and children relate well to them. Just seeing you try to be humorous lets them know that you have a sense of humor and care about trying to make your teaching more enjoyable! Remember to check out the appendix for many more jokes and ideas to incorporate into your newly creative teaching. And certainly, always keep this quote in mind:

> Not only does a smile cost less than electricity, it also *brightens your day*.
> —Author Unknown

We will leave you a poignant thought by my friend, Ralph Marston. He has allowed me to use his inspirational quotes and passages in my books, from his "Daily Motivator." He has so many wonderful ideas that he shares with others! When time, go to www.greatday.com to make whatever you are facing seem not so concerning or overwhelming.

Sadness

> *In every life there is some sadness.* The loss of a loved one, the disappointment of a shattered dream. Things don't always go the way we want.
>
> Sadness hurts. It is difficult. And ultimately, it is good. Because sadness can come only when you care. As painful as it is, consider the alternative. What if you did not even care? Paradoxically, the *absence of pain is the ultimate pain.*
>
> We must learn to experience and appreciate our sadness, *without being overwhelmed by it.* And the first step is to admit it and feel it for what it is. It is a powerful *form of caring.* About ourselves, about others, about truth, about love, about life. Sadness shows us how very much we care, and defines for us the truly important things in life.
>
> *Even in the pain of sadness, there is meaning and hope.* Out of sadness, comes a deeper sense of appreciation. The sunshine is more precious after a week of rainy days. In sadness is the strength to go forward and the *opportunity to triumph* over every obstacle.[13]
> — Ralph Marston

Well, chapter 5 has finally arrived, the "true heart" of teaching: "Using Humor with Techniques for Better Classroom Management!" You might want to jot down a few ideas.

NOTES

1. Dalai Lama, Howard Cutler, and Richard Davidson, *The Art of Happiness* (New York, Riverbend Books, 2009).

2. Lynne Namka, *Step Back and Breathe: Lesson Plans for Teaching Anger Management to Children* (Amazon Digital Services, 2014).

3. Daniel Goleman, "Emotional Intelligence," http://www.danielgoleman .info/topics/emotional-intelligence/.

4. National Association of School Psychologists, "Helping Children Cope with Loss, Death, and Grief," http://www.nasponline.org/assets/documents/Resources%20and%20Publications/Handouts/Safety%20and%20Crisis/Grief-War.pdf (PDF).

5. Ibid.

6. Adapted from material first posted on the National Association of School Psychologists (NASP) website after September 11, 2001. NASP has made these materials available free of charge to the public in order to promote the ability of children and youth to cope with traumatic or unsettling times. National Association of School Psychologists, "Helping Children Cope with Loss, Death, and Grief Tips for Teachers and Parents," http://www.nasponline .org/assets/documents/Resources%20and%20Publications/Handouts/Safety%20and%20Crisis/GriefWar.pdf.

7. Lynne Namka, *Step Back and Breathe: Lesson Plans for Teaching Anger Management to Children* (Amazon Digital Services, 2014).

8. Lawrence Robinson, Jeanne Segal, and Melinda Smith, "Managing Conflicts with Humor," helpguide.org, https://www.helpguide.org/articles/relationships-communication/managing-conflicts-with-humor.htm.

9. Ibid.

10. Ibid.

11. http://www.jokes4us.com/knockknockjokes/knockknockfoodjokes.html

12. http://www.jokes4us.com/animaljokes/dinosaurjokes.html

13. Ralph Marston, "Sadness," *The Daily Motivator*, Monday, March 24, 1997. (www.greatday.com)

5

USING HUMOR WITH TECHNIQUES FOR BETTER CLASSROOM MANAGEMENT

PROVEN "MAGICAL CLASSROOM MANAGEMENT" STRATEGIES THAT WORK!

Here is a little humor to begin this chapter:

> Good teachers are the ones who can challenge young minds without losing their own!
>
> —D. Martin

The following sections are adapted from California Risk Management Authority, "Classroom Management Techniques to Reduce Student Discipline," Safety Matters newsletter. [1]

Establish Classroom Rules on the First Day and Enforce Them Consistently

If possible, try to make a *humorous PowerPoint presentation* to show with examples. Some teachers are more comfortable making a chart, which can be left up in the classroom for several days for their students to see. The visual aids will help children with short attention spans, and, as we all have heard, "a picture is worth a thousand words." In addition, they both can be used year after year and are helpful if the class needs a review of the rules from time to time.

> Strength is the capacity to break a chocolate bar into four pieces with your bare hands—and then eat just one of the pieces.
>
> —Judith Viorist

Establish rules on the first day of class, and always follow through on the specified rewards for achievement and consequences for misbehavior. Consistency is so important! (Let the class know you, as a teacher, have rules that take strength to follow, too!) If you allow a student to get away with misbehavior without consequence even once, you've opened the door to future misbehavior and negotiation of rules. This is particularly important at the beginning of the year, when you're building your students' trust in you as their teacher.[2]

Use humor to correct poor behaviors, like saying: "Yikers, which rule are you already forgetting?" (You might need to give many hints for some students!) Say, "Even if it is the first day, 'Picky Teacher Me' must insist you follow all rules! We must be fair to everyone. If you do 'the crime,' you must give me some time! Besides, this way you will be helping to remind the others before they break the same rule . . . and we know they might! Right?"

Let the class guess at what rules they expect to be on the list, just to get them thinking and participating. Sometimes they can even make half of the rules, so they take ownership.

Using humor and examples children understand will help everyone to enjoy their learning process, and the parents will appreciate you even more!

Let Children Take Ownership of Their Own Behavior, Even if They Don't Want It

Set *logical rules* and consequences for good and bad behavior using a PowerPoint presentation or wall chart with emphasis on rewards. Keep the goal of learning in mind, and make sure students know why the rules are what they are: You can say, "We walk instead of running in the hallway, because we want to make sure that YOU do not run over the teachers, and we all want to be safe and not squished!" (Wait for the giggles.) Say, "Can you imagine if all the teachers, parents, and even our principal ran where they were going? Sort of funny to think about, though, right?"

And always fit the consequence to "the crime." If a student makes a giant mess of the art supplies, the logical consequence is to clean it up.[3] And not by another student or the teacher! Say something like, "Oh no, a wild hurricane or tornado must have hit our art center! Maybe you got in a hurry with your masterpiece, and now can go back and straighten things up?"

Arbitrary punishments like losing recess, or something else unrelated to the offense, teach students that you are a "meanie" and perhaps trying to force a power struggle.[4] The children who usually cause most of the problems need an "energy release" like recess, more than ever!

A positive way to show team effort and how to be a team player is to use the "team point system" and it is reflective of the "competitive spirit" many children seem to possess and love. An important thing to always remember as a teacher or parent is: *competition is great if the goal is possible for all!*

Each class is divided into table teams, identified by numbers or the names they choose as a group, changing members each week. No one wants the "rule follower" to say, "But Sam is messy and never gets us any points, we don't want him on our team!" To avoid this, make sure to shuffle the kids, so "good role models" are separated out; making certain one is on each team. That way, the children are confused as to why they get points often, or don't get as many as the last time the points were added up. (Aren't we teachers tricky?) The points are tallied at the end of the week, or day, with a simple reward for the winning team. For example, ten minutes of extra recess or free time at the play station. Some will be happy to have ten minutes to draw or just read their book!

Another way to show immediate reward is to say, "Put a sticker up by your name on the sticker chart for being so kind to Jenny!" Sometimes teachers have a simple prize box that winners can select from as well. The rewards are important, but not nearly as important, as how the child feels being appreciated by others and putting up their own star or point. This exercise also aids in learning how to neatly tally by 5s. By the way, they love counting by 5s!

Enable Children to Feel Responsible for Their Best Learning Environment

Use humor to discuss how and why it is so important to have each student feel *responsible*. Give your students power over their learning environment, which helps them to feel responsible for their own learning. Create rules together as a class, demonstrating humorous "right and wrong" examples. Encourage those with good leadership personalities to direct the in-class discussion, or better yet, have them act out some role-play.

Make certain to walk around instead of standing up front for the entire lesson. You do not want to be the "dictator of conversation." Ask students to "monitor" themselves, as in "Check yourself to see if you are using your indoor voice," while showing them a very "Loud Voice of the Teacher" as an outdoor voice. This will send the message that you see the students as individuals who are *capable* of handling themselves.

Positive reminders work wonders! Like, "Michele, today you are acting like a 'Rock Star' in your leadership and learning. Can I have your autograph?" This will make everyone smile, wanting to be the next "Rock Star." Explain how it is so important for everyone to take *pride and participate* in their class. Or let them read this up on the board:

> If your absence won't make any difference, *neither* will your presence!
> —Author unknown

DESIRED BEHAVIORS MUST BE FOR THE GOOD OF THE CHILD, NOT THE TEACHER

> I think a secure profession for young people is history teacher, because in the future, there will be so much more of it to teach.
> —Bill Muse

Use humor, and always praise efforts and achievements for their own sake, and *not* for the sake of teacher approval. Give constant feedback about good behaviors: "I notice that 'Magical Margo' has her History book out and is ready to go. Now her whole row is ready to gain a point for their team! I bet the other teams are getting a little worried? If not . . . *Maybe they should be!*"

But keep the emphasis on the behavior, not on the teacher's approval. Avoid saying, "I like how . . ." *because it doesn't matter what the teacher likes.* Right?[5]

It might be hard for us to realize that students shouldn't do things to please the teacher; they should do things because they are the "right things to do," resulting in a good feeling of leadership for all. Say, "How many of you have played 'follow the leader'? Let's try it! 'Leader Linda,' can you show the others how you just did that? You are so amazing; some day you just might be our president!"

Positive Humorous Reinforcement Is Key

Always use positive instead of negative language. A "spoonful of sugar makes the medicine go down." Sounds sort of dumb to us, but children *can relate* easily to this cliché.

We all have noticed that as soon as you tell children *not* to do something, the first image in that child's brain is what you said not to do. For example: "Don't think about cats hissing at you!" Are you immediately thinking about hissing cats? Thought so.

To avoid the annoying subconscious, opt for silly positive-language, instead of negative-language rules. For example:

"Always be prepared for our *Fun School Zone*" instead of "Don't forget your homework again!"

"Please move your chair quietly like a *Sneaky Burglar*" instead of "Don't scrape your chair so often!"

"Always listen politely to your *Terrific Teacher and Perfect Peers*" instead of "Don't talk while others are talking; it's rude!"

Use the words "Creepy Consequences" instead of the extremely negative "punishments." Reinforce that it is "their choice," not the "Terrific Teacher's" or "Perfect Peer's" fault, to choose the behavior which leads to "Cool Consequences" or "Creepy Consequences."

Teaching and Management Style Must Be Developmentally Appropriate for Every Child

> Please excuse the mess, we are busy learning with joy!
> —Author unknown

We know that not all students learn at the same pace. Guess what? Neither do adults! (Let children know this, too!) Taking more time to do a good job is always okay. Take the time to make sure everyone is "on board" when explaining how the room can be when learning as a group. Productive noise can help us learn. Children love knowing that we all learn at different rates, and that even our parents are the same with learning new things. Remember, verbally for them, the times that *you had a hard time* learning something new in recent years.

Perhaps it was taking up skiing, or even learning how to navigate around your new computer or smartphone? Smartphones tend to be smarter than most of us, anyway! Explain to them how frustrating it might have been and what you did to master it. (Do not tell them if you gave up or quit! Please.)

Always stick with those who don't understand the topic and check in with them regularly to help them keep up to speed. The last thing you want is for them to glaze over; choosing to give up. It is imperative for the teacher *not* to get frantically frustrated and act out in response. Our job as parents and teachers is to be kind, caring, and understanding of skill levels in each child we work with.

On the flip side, we know bored students can cause problems daily. Make sure that you are challenging the students who move more quickly through the material by overplanning and preparing extra, quiet activities.

For example, if a student has finished the math assignment with twenty minutes to spare, challenge him or her to step up to the next level designed for "Hot Shots in Math Club"! You can introduce a difficult math word problem for such students, and provide a clean piece of paper for them to show how they found the answer. Points are given for their team. The Point System encourages "team player" behavior in the class.

And the best part is that points can be earned for anything, and by all students. This includes those, at the very least, "just trying hard to finish"! Explain that they can even get points for neatness, great attitudes, helping others, picking up trash, smiling nicely at the teacher, and so on. When you are silly, they can enjoy trying more often, and they soon realize that points are not only earned for academic endeavors.

Unfortunately, many children get used to feeling "less than" with their first school experience. This can happen due to their peers, bullies, and other people not even realizing they are doing it. *Self-esteem is paramount* for a child to even want to come to school and learn, and as teachers and parents, it is our pleasure to ensure our children get the chance to always feel "worthy" with an attitude to at least give their best effort.

Confrontations Are Wasted Negative Energy

> Only two things are infinite, the universe and human stupidity, and I'm not sure about the former.
>
> —Albert Einstein.

We are sure Einstein was referring to those who bully or humiliate others!

Please avoid confrontations in front of students at all costs. This is so important to be a successful teacher. Count to ten if you must, but take the high road. Humor can always work wonders to help defuse many problems!

Additionally, using a little humor with students when pointing out their poor behavior and how it affects their own learning as well as others' might take some of the "sting" away. It is never a good idea to make an example of a student by shaming him or her in front of his or her peers. If you're dealing with a misbehavior, speak to the student in the hallway or after class to resolve the issue instead of allowing an in-class confrontation.[6] Avoiding "power plays" cannot be overemphasized.

> Teachers are the only professionals who have to respond to bells every forty-five minutes and come out fighting.
>
> —Frank McCourt

However, at the elementary grade level, the fighting is mostly outside during recess!

The Perfect Book for Those Who Have Many Bad Days

We have all had some extraordinary days, when we feel all the universe is going in the correct direction just to make our day perfect! But we also have experienced days we wish we could go back to bed and *begin again*, right?

Remember the quote from Jacob Nordby: "Blessed are the weird people—poets, misfits, writers, mystics, painters, and troubadours—for they teach us to see the world through different eyes." Some of today's geniuses and those of the past were probably once considered "weird."

Let children know that "We all have bad days, or make bad choices, but it is *not* the end of the world!" In chapter 2, we mentioned some great books for third-graders. One is *Doctor De Soto*, another is *Danny Dinosaur*, and the third one is *Runny Babbit*! Well, another one of the best for all children to read or have read to them is described below.

Think of a time you as a teacher, or when you were a child, were having a very bad day. Give examples you remember, and then read the funny book *Alexander and the Terrible, Horrible, No Good, Very Bad Day*, by Judith Viorst. (Even older children find this book funny!)

Here is a little taste of Alexander's terrible day: From the moment Alexander wakes up things just do not go his way. As he gets up, the horror begins. He spills milk on the floor and Philip Parker has arranged for a birthday party the same evening as Alexander but things start to go his way.

In the carpool on the way to school, he doesn't get a window seat. His teacher, Mrs. Dickens, doesn't like his picture of the invisible castle (which is actually just a blank sheet of paper), criticizes him for singing too loud, and publicly scolds him for skipping the number 16 at counting time. His friend, Paul, deserts him for his third best friend and there is no dessert in his lunch bag.

The dentist tells him he has a cavity and he must come back next week so it can be fixed; the elevator door closes on his foot; Anthony pushes him into a mud puddle; Nick says he is a crybaby; when he punches Nick in response, their mother punishes him for being muddy and for trying to punch Nick.

At the shoe store, they're out of Alexander's choice of sneakers (blue ones with red stripes), so his mother has to buy him plain white ones, which he refuses to wear. At his father's office, he makes a mess of things when he fools around with everything there (the copying machine, the books, and the telephone), getting to the point where his dad tells the family not to pick him up anymore.

At home, they have lima beans for dinner (which he hates); there is kissing on TV (which he also hates); bath time becomes a nightmare (the water being too hot, getting soap in his eyes, and his marble going down the drain); and he must wear his railroad train pajamas (which he also hates). At bedtime, his night-light burns out; he bites his tongue; Nick takes back a pillow he said he could keep; and the cat chooses to sleep with Anthony.

A running gag throughout the book is Alexander repeating several times that he wants to move to Australia because he thinks it's better there. It ends with his mother's assurance that everybody has bad days, even those who live there in Australia.[7] In the Australian and New Zealand versions, he wants to move to Timbuktu instead (presumably because he already lives in Australia).

After reading the book to your class, take the time for discussion of bad days we all have had at one time or another. This book could be used as an amazing writing prompt; and then let each child who wants to come up in the "Author's Chair" to share.

Parent Involvement Is Magical to Better Management

> Dear Parents: If you promise not to believe everything your child says happens at school, I'll promise not to believe everything he says happens at home.
>
> —Author unknown

Send Home Humorous Weekly Newsletters

Connect with the parents, grandparents, caregivers, and children by sending home a weekly funny newsletter. The child will be more eager to have their parent read it, and more likely to bring it home.

After school begins, send a sincere, yet humorous note like this:

Date _____

Guess what Mom and Dad?

I lived through my first week of school. My teacher says, "I survived as well!" I am really not sure what she means; do YOU? In reality, I have to do all the work! She just tells us lots of stuff to do each day, and even gives us homework!

Who knew there would be so many rules to follow in school? There are tons of them, like: Rules in the Room, Rules for the Outside, Rules for the Play Equipment, Rules for the Gym, Rules for the Halls, Rules for the Cafeteria, Rules for the Bus, and even Rules for the Bathroom!

Good thing we do not have so many rules at home. I am sure I am forgetting some of the rules she has told us about. But ask me if I remember any of them by reminding me the different school areas. I guess rules are important for safety, and so that everyone can enjoy their time at school. I never thought about that. Some of the more important rules are attached for you to quiz me on.

My teacher understands that dreams we have come in all shapes and sizes, and she wants me to tell you why some of my dreams come so large:

"Dreams come a size too big so that we can grow into them." —
Josie Bisset

Regardless of all the rules, I am liking my teacher _____, and she/he has funny things in the daily lessons. Ask me for an example of a "Knock-Knock joke" that I heard in math. She/he tells us that it is the best way to get us to listen and pay attention. She/he is oh, so right! Just about the time I begin daydreaming, or wishing recess would come, she/he says something funny and I find myself more interested in what she has to say! I wonder why that is?

Some times when we get very wiggly we just do "jumping jacks" or some other movement games like skipping and sit-ups. One day we even did something called "quiet meditation." I think the word was "yoga"? Wow, was that a quiet, peaceful time! We are all surprised how much more easily we can settle down, plus I get so much more done. My teacher is sort of "Magical" that way! One day when it was extra noisy before a test, the teacher put on "thinking music," as it was called, and what a difference that made!

Well, that's about all for now . . . but look at the second page for upcoming events, and things we will be learning more about next week. You might remind me to do my homework that is attached too. Thanks for reading this.

Your brilliant, kind, funny, caring child _____

And his humorous teacher, _____

Let children and parents know how important attitude is when it comes to learning new things and getting along with others . . . we can say, *"You can't be a smart cookie if you have a crumby attitude." —Author Unknown*

If you have the opportunity, make a friendly phone call to set the stage for a successful school year. This can be done prior to school beginning as an introduction of yourself, and a way to find out important information concerning your students (allergies, divorce, worries, passions, learning difficulties, etc.).

By using some humor, you will make the parent as well as their children feel relaxed and less intimidated. Having the support of your students and their parents can help determine how your year will unfold. If allowed, they can be your "Helpful Heroes," saving you hours of time, stress, and even spending money! Many parents are happy to help supply things, if they like you. You just have to ask.

The wise teacher knows that 55 minutes of work plus 5 minutes laughter are worth twice as much as 60 minutes of unvaried work.

—Gilbert Highet

Contact Parents Early and Often

Send weekly updates as to what is needed in the classroom, and what things are being learned. A line or two of something funny, even a joke to read to their child, will make both student and parent want to read the "Weekly Wishes" as soon as they arrive home! By being just a little clever, your news will not end up in the "oval file," otherwise known as the garbage can!

Encourage attendance at parent–teacher "Complimentary Conferences." (We called them "bragging conferences," since all students have strengths in some way for us to compliment.) Let your students know the meeting will be held mainly to "show parents all their good work" but also to show Mom or Dad what you might need more help understanding. This quote can get a giggle out of most parents and some children:

> The only place success comes before work is in the dictionary.
> —Vince Lombardi

After sharing this quote, show students the literal truth of the statement, using a dictionary, to make the learning more meaningful. See how many in your class even know how to use a dictionary correctly, as that can be a real eye-opener!

Have a fun contest to get 100 percent of your class and their parents to attend! They will love the excitement of trying to reach their goal. Have them determine and vote on the reasonable reward (ice-cream party, longer recess for a few days, or a special appropriate movie).

Always demonstrate that you want to work with the parents to instruct their children to the very best of your ability. Make sure they feel your caring for each and every student, even the "troublemaker" of the class. If you develop a good relationship with the parents, you'll open a dialogue among parent, student, and teacher that allows for a freer flow of feedback—and it always helps to have a sense of humor, which adds to everyone's comfort level and usually gains the parents' support.[8]

> The work can wait while you show the child the rainbow, but the rainbow won't wait while you do the work.
> —Patricia Clafford

Use "Humorous Show and Tell" by Interactively Modeling Behaviors

The first time you do something, show the students how to do it. Using puppetry, illustration, and "role play" with children works wonders! Then ask them to share what they noticed about what you did. Ask a student to do it, and discuss that action with the class. When you as a teacher take the time to plan a lesson or activity that will engage and entertain the students, you become more than just their teacher . . . you can become their "hero."

Why not have them again show the "right and wrong" way to accomplish something for humorous comparisons? Lastly, have the whole class practice. The "having fun with it" will be longer lasting for the children, and now the brain has a fun "visual" remember, aiding retention.

If you go slow the first time, you'll be able to go faster later with the confidence that all the students know *how to perform* the action the right way.

Slow and steady wins the race!

"Ready, Set . . . No? Then We Will Wait for YOU!"

Make sure you get the attention of every student before beginning class.[9] It is obvious that some children just take longer to be ready . . . for anything! We as teachers and parents need to give them that time. Sometimes it is called giving a student "wait time" for readiness, giving an answer, or the relaxed feeling that comes from the calmness many students need to begin.

Remember it is always better to start slowly than to begin a lesson with some students looking out the window or daydreaming about recess! We might have heard, "To survive as a teacher you need three bones: a wishbone, a backbone, and a funny bone" (Author unknown).

This doesn't require yelling "Be quiet, sit down, class is beginning"—in fact, that's almost sure to be disastrous. Instead, stand silent and wait until the students "shush each other" and settle down. Perhaps have them learn the Peace Sign or two fingers up to indicate "Quiet." Or if that's not your style, redirect the beginning-of-class chatter by turning the lights off, then on. Sometimes a type of clicker that is easily heard can stop the talking so that they look at you.

Since everyone can notice the lights going off over a bell or whistle, a consistent signal like that is easier than searching for your little bell or clicker. Of course, the meaning has to be established first. The "Listening Lights" lets all students notice that talking is to cease and attention is to be given immediately!

Throwing out an untrue engaging question, comment, or observation can capture attention: "Hey, I heard today is Free Ice-Cream Day! Is that true?" Once you have everyone's attention, say, "See, even teachers can start rumors!" (Explain what a rumor is for the younger child, then giggle and proceed with the day's fun lesson plan.)

Movement is Magical for Management and Brain Stimulation

Use proximity and directness to your advantage![10] If students are mis-
behaving in class, it's smart to take a stretch break or do a few jumping
jacks. (The teacher may need them more than the student, as we all can
imagine). *Oxygen to the brain is phenomenal.*

Or if just one student is having issues, continue your lesson but walk
over and stand next to him or her, and ask the student to help you do
something. Say something like, "Hey, Victor . . . Can you hold my book
while I get the pencils?" Having a teacher so close usually shuts down
students' misbehavior without embarrassing them. You can also use a
direct question to snap a student back into the lesson like: "Mark, why
do you think 'Chicken Little' is so concerned? Have you ever felt that
way? When?" Be sure to start the call-out with the student's name so
that he or she hears the full question. If the student really cannot
answer, ask someone else to help.[11]

End adaptation.

Make Learning Simple, Meaningful, and Fun!

Humor and consistent organization are paramount. Children like to
know what to expect, and so being organized while making learning fun
keeps them wanting to come to school. That is huge when you consider
how much some children skip school.

Structure, both within a lesson and throughout the month, will help
your students stay on top of their work. Write the day's activities on the
board before class. Always put some funny assignment or silly question
on the list, to get them eager to read what they are to do every day!
(e.g., write: When you finish #4 on this list, Stand Up and Smile at Your
Terrific Teacher!)

After giving them some time to read directions silently, choose readers to read the list aloud. This is a great activity to practice reading
directions, and making sure everyone knows what they are to do for the
work. For a change, say, "Who wants to read our directions *backward*?"
After the hands of your great readers shoot into the air and you select a
"star reader" to start reading the list, say, "No, 'backward' means you
have to turn around so you cannot see them!" They love these silly
comments. In addition, they listen more.

Remember to send home a "calendar of FUN learning" for parents and children at the beginning of the month and stick to it; if you get off track, provide a revised calendar, so that students and parents always know where they are in the class. You can call it your "exciting road map to learning!"

During class, be prepared for each ensuing activity; lag time wastes both your and your students' time . . . and introduces boredom or behavioral problems into the classroom. Who wants that?[12]

Now that you have seen a variety of ways to use humor or silly comments in your own management style of the classroom, doesn't a class filled with fun and humor sound like a room you would like to be in for the day, or have your child be a part of?

If you are thinking, "Well, I do not think of myself as funny or even humorous," then get some joke books from the library. You can scan some pages to put on an overhead for the children to enjoy upon starting a new topic. Before you can say "Jack Robinson" you will be humorous too! Always remember, the sillier the better for the young children, and simple knock-knock jokes and riddles are loved by all.

HOW TO BRING LAUGHTER INTO YOUR LESSONS WITH THREE MAJOR GUIDES: COMEDY FROM PAIN?

Sounds odd, but did you know that a great deal of comedy comes from pain? Nothing is as it seems, so to laugh is the way we deal with adversity. If you aren't comfortable with confronting your pain, then none of this will work.

It can be hard as a teacher when you hear your students making fun of you. Even though it can sting a little, it is best to address the issue in front of the class by making a joke. For example if a student is making fun of your outfit, you can always say "you should have seen the goofy outfits I wore in high school!" Students will learn they can be comfortable with you and that insulting or condescending tones aren't needed in the classroom. Lisa Chesser, in her article "Comedy in the Classroom: 50 Ways to Bring Laughter Into Any Lesson," has these suggestions:

- Establish rapport

- Lighten up
- Be weird
- Use voices
- Be gross (but only to a limit!)
- Be messy
- Share your feelings
- Heal wounds
- Make and break rules
- Do charades
- Discuss reality TV
- Give false consequences
- Use situational comedy
- Use sarcasm
- Use antics
- Challenge flaws
- Use hope
- Switch places with your students
- List your worst moments
- Ask about superheroes
- Just say "Seriously?"
- Catch silly lies
- Turn out the lights[13]

"Laughter is an amazing tool. It is often forgotten as kids get older and more serious studies take over. We all hope that our children's teachers can remember that you can't teach someone something if you haven't reached them . . . and laughter is a great way to touch someone."[14]

Humor connects everyone in the classroom. And although it takes selective teachers to know which humorous strategies are grade-level appropriate for the children they work with, once chosen correctly, teachers will have "magical tools of humor" that will speak the language the child speaks!

We truly believe in the "power of humor" in the classroom! Unfortunately, though, just as not everyone is a comedian, it's really hard to expect every teacher to leverage humor. We also know, however, while not everyone is a comedian, some of the suggestions here are more practical and conversational as opposed to laugh-out-loud slapstick.

This book hopes most teachers see these suggestions as ways to connect with their students. We like the embarrassing story or "gross" tactics too, because often they're a great way of pulling children into a story and getting them to interact without realizing they're doing it.

Many teachers worry that being "funny" or "strange" will mean they lose their authority, but you can have a balance of the two. Children are more likely to respond to you if they like you.

A primary teacher used humor with juggling to capture the imagination of her classes: "I used to love teachers at my primary school who could, effectively, be a bit of an idiot. In a good way; all the slapstick stuff, being weird, showing off with unusual tricks. I'd recommend any teacher to learn the basics of juggling—the three-ball cascade is easy to master and it'll wow your class. They'll think you're a magician! You could take it a step further and learn some additional magic tricks. Keeping up to date with all the latest trends won't do you any harm, either."[15]

Many clever teachers "not only juggle, but teach the students to juggle as part of a lesson in middle school. The kids were juggling all kinds of things and practicing the lesson to perfection. And, magic, what a great way to teach concepts!"[16]

The students are fascinated and totally engaged, which can be a superb opening to teach a new lesson. Eye-hand coordination is a weakness in many children, so juggling can develop these important skills necessary for handwriting, drawing, and many different sports.

As a teacher or parent even taking the time to read this book, we are sure you use many good techniques already, but now you have even more tools to try out. We believe students should laugh, have fun, and enjoy school while learning, don't you?

Another thing to keep in mind is that a "video really breaks up a lesson that may be difficult or even boring."[17] Show classroom videos of silly faces and actions of students involved with science experiments, reading their story, or telling something new they learned outside of school. Miss. Whimsy says, "I think incorporating a little humor into the classroom is a win-win situation. Knowing and understanding your students is super important. I use humor to keep kids on their toes. If I even think for a second one of my little ones is losing focus I might just test them by saying 'candy!' and see if I get a smile (or better eye contact!) from anyone."[18]

She continues, "I am also a firm believer in varying your voice every now and then. Sometimes I will whisper parts of my lesson to "reel" kids back into the lesson/story/etc."[19] Most teachers get laryngitis and lose their voice once a year, and this whispering technique can save your voice. Who knew you could also get their sympathy, plus more engagement with what you are teaching at the same time!

Try to get excited and dramatic when reading books, primarily because it keeps kids engaged! If you are excited, kids will be excited too (or they will at least be intrigued and wonder why in the world their teacher is so weird or hyper).[20] Many times, changing the book or play character's names to those of children in the class will get better attention, and giggles for sure! The teacher can even substitute his or her own name for laughs.

Hopefully, like her, we all have "fond memories of teachers who would incorporate a laugh or two during the day."[21] Those are the educators who know how to relax and gain trust from their students. It's hard to sit still and keep engaged—a little humor once in a while just makes children respect a teacher even more, because it's almost like the teacher "gets" that school can be monotonous sometimes.

Connecting learning skills to something in students' lives they can relate to will work wonders. Once students make that connection, learning something new became easier and more fun.[22] Here is a comment from someone who remembers "that teacher" who was funny and knew how to connect with his high-school students.

> I remember one teacher from high school so well because he was "that teacher." The fondest memory I have of high school was from his class (Geography, boooo!). The lights were halfway off and we were supposed to be taking notes, but I guess he noticed all of our eyes glaze over because the next thing I knew he was saying "Off to town go Mom and Pop. The ox can help! Hop on top!"
>
> We had no idea he had been talking about the Big Blue Ox, but I promise we paid attention after that, because we knew he would catch us. He was a hilarious teacher and one of the few that the kids liked so much that no one wanted to misbehave, not out of fear, but out of respect.[23]

When a teacher can gain the trust and respect of students, the learning will not stop, but will instead be a journey of loving education.

HUMOROUS TEACHERS ARE HARD TO FORGET

As a teacher from so many years ago, this author remembers a teacher in college everyone wanted during registration. He taught history in such a fun and meaningful way; he had humorous stories still remembered today. All the details of the dates were not as important as being able to understand some of the reasons historical events happened in the first place. And fortunately for us, he made some of them hysterical!

"Pam Schiller and Clarissa A. Willis, both PhD authors, speakers, and curriculum specialists, note that laughter not only increases one's capacity to remember the humor, but also provides a feeling of security and contentment, both of which enhance learning and retention."[24]

Increase Your Odds at the Interview as a New Teacher

Job interviews require you to be professional, but that shouldn't exclude the use of some clever levity. Most hiring managers are drawn to job candidates who know how to put others at ease with a knack of humor; it's usually associated, as we now know, with an offered contract. It may take a while to develop a comfortable way to use humor in your job, but it's a worthy pursuit.

The goal isn't to be voted "funniest teacher," or force yourself to be someone you're not. By being aware of the benefits of adding some wittiness to your own "brand," you'll likely accelerate your standing with your students, their parents, and of course your principal![25]

Hopefully now you have written down a few ideas that you would feel comfortable trying at home or in the classroom. Just looking through the appendix will give you some ideas, and certainly either make you groan or laugh out loud!

NOTES

1. California Risk Management Authority, "Classroom Management Techniques to Reduce Student Discipline," Safety Matters newsletter, https://www.madera.k12.ca.us/site/handlers/filedownload.ashx?moduleinstanceid=5591&dataid=15688&FileName=December%202016%20Safety%20Newsletter.pdf.

2. Ibid.

3. Ibid.

4. Ibid.

5. Ibid.

6. Ibid.

7. Judith Viorist, *Alexander and the Terrible, Horrible, No Good, Very Bad Day*, illustrated by Ray Cruz (New York: Atheneum, 1972).

8. California Risk Management Authority, "Classroom Management Techniques to Reduce Student Discipline."

9. Ibid.

10. Ibid.

11. Ibid.

12. Ibid.

13. Linda Chesser, "Comedy in the Classroom: 50 Ways to Bring Laughter Into Any Lesson," https://www.opencolleges.edu.au/informed/features/comedy-in-the-classroom-50-ways-to-bring-laughter-into-any-lesson/

14. Ibid.

15. Alex at Office Kitten, comment on Chesser, "Comedy in the Classroom," March 29, 2013.

16. Lisa Chesser, comment on Chesser, "Comedy in the Classroom," March 31, 2013.

17. Lisa Chesser, comment on Chesser, "Comedy in the Classroom," March 31, 2013.

18. Miss. Whimsy, comment on Chesser, "Comedy in the Classroom," March 30, 2013.

19. Ibid.

20. Ibid.

21. Ibid.

22. Pat, comment on Chesser, "Comedy in the Classroom," April 2, 2013.

23. Lacy, comment on Chesser, "Comedy in the Classroom," May 1, 2013.

24. Saga Briggs, "15 Surprising Discoveries about Learning," https://www.opencolleges.edu.au/informed/features/15-surprising-discoveries-about-learning/.

25. Lynn Taylor, "Add Humor to Your Job and Boost Your Career: A Little Levity Can Go a Long Way at Work," 2015, https://www.psychologytoday.com/us/blog/tame-your-terrible-office-tyrant/201504/add-humor-your-job-and-boost-your-career.

6

HUMOR IS THE KEY TO CLASSROOM MANAGEMENT, PARENTAL INVOLVEMENT, AND RETENTION OF INFORMATION FOR CHILDREN

CREATE OPPORTUNITIES TO LAUGH IN THE CLASSROOM, FACULTY ROOM, OR AT HOME NOW!

Deja Poo: The feeling a teacher gets at a faculty meeting that she's heard this stuff before.

—Heidi McDonald

As you have probably already discovered,

Shared laughter is one of the most effective tools for keeping relationships fresh and exciting. All emotional sharing builds strong and lasting relationship bonds, but sharing laughter also adds joy, vitality, and resilience. And humor is a powerful and effective way to heal resentments, disagreements, and hurts. Laughter unites people during difficult times. [1]

Here are some ideas to use in *your classroom, home, or faculty room* to create much-needed laughs daily:

- Read a funny book to your children often.
- Seek out funny people to speak to your class.
- Share a good joke or a funny story daily.

- Check out your bookstore's or library's humor section.
- Have fun "learning games" available.
- Play with a pet in your class or at home.
- Watch a learning video that has humor.
- Give children time to learn using puppetry and role play.
- Play around with children inside and outside.
- Do something silly, even if you are not a silly person.
- Make time for fun activities (e.g. baseball, bowling, miniature golfing, karaoke).[2]

By incorporating more humor and play into your daily interactions can improve the quality of your love relationships . . . as well as your connections with coworkers, family members, and friends. Using humor and laughter in relationships allows you to:

1. **Be More Spontaneous.** Humor gets you out of your head and away from your troubles.
2. **Let Go of Defensiveness.** Laughter helps you forget resentments, judgments, criticisms, and doubts.
3. **Release Inhibitions.** Your fear of holding back and holding on are set aside.
4. **Express Your True Feelings.** Deeply felt emotions are allowed to rise to the surface.[3]

BRING MORE HUMOR AND LAUGHTER INTO YOUR LIFE

Teachers usually love what they do, and using humor in the lessons makes the day go faster, and the children more involved and engaged with what they are learning. Tell them:

> Warning! I'm a teacher. I'll always be young at heart. I'll never grow up and act my age.
>
> —Heidi McDonald

What is funny at a very young age does not stay very humorous. For instance, as What to Expect puts it,

> Putting a pair of underwear on your head may not get many giggles at a grown-up dinner party, but if you're entertaining a table full of

toddlers, few sight gags are more effective. No spare undies? Stick a few straws in your ears or hang a spoon from your nose for a guaranteed giggle fest.

You might not realize it, but your goofiness is not just a laughing matter: Each silly situation helps your toddler develop a sense of humor, something that has to be nurtured since it's not inherited. So when do toddlers start laughing at funny things? At around 14 to 15 months, they're able to understand that funny faces and illogical acts are meant to be laughed at. When you do something obviously silly, like pretend to eat off the plate as a dog would, it's particularly pleasing for your pipsqueak because he's sure that's not what's supposed to happen, and being sure is a great feeling for a toddler who's still unsure about so much of what he experiences.[4]

Remember, "Silliness makes your soul smile." —Doe Zantamata

As they're developing a sense of humor, toddlers also appreciate funny physical feats, especially the kind with an element of surprise, like peekaboo and unexpected tickles. Or you can knock yourself on the head with a pillow and pretend to fall over—any sort of slapstick does the trick.[5]

Again, so dumb to us, while genius to a young child!

And once their language skills have blossomed, they'll find rhymes and nonsense words funny too. Your toddler may also try making you laugh, perhaps by using your hairbrush as a cell phone, for instance. At around 24 months, he may point to his elbow when you say, "Show me your nose," or pick up a doll and call it a truck, simply to get a giggle out of you. And he'll redo his stand-up routine again and again and again.[6]

If you have ever taught Kindergarten you will like this one:

When I see the mind of the five-year-old, I see a volcano with two vents: destructiveness and creativeness.

—Sylvia Ashton-Warner

Naturally, the jokes may get old, but your laugh will boost his comic confidence, so don't skimp on the snickers. Soon she'll start to anticipate humor, so if you're the one repeating jokes, you may find your child chuckling before the punch line. It's all good.

In chapter 3, we discussed the connection between humor and developing self-esteem, which leads to better learning and a more enjoyable life! So, let's get giggling!

Want More Laughter in Your Life and in your Classroom? Get a Pet

Most of us have experienced the joy of playing with a furry friend, and pets are a rewarding way to bring more laughter and joy into your life. But did you know that having a pet is good for your mental and physical health? Studies show that *pets can protect you, and lessen depression, stress, and even heart disease. In essence, many live longer who have a critter to love.* [7]

> If you've ever owned a pet, you already know how much fun and affection they can bring. But did you know that pets also come with some pretty powerful mental and physical health benefits? Dogs in particular can reduce stress, anxiety, and depression, ease loneliness, encourage exercise and playfulness, and even improve your cardiovascular health. Caring for a dog can help children grow up more secure and active or provide valuable companionship for older adults. Perhaps most importantly, though, a dog can add real joy and unconditional love to your life. [8]

Wouldn't it be wonderful if all children could have some type of a pet? However, we also know some living arrangements are not conducive to doing so. With this being the case, it is even more important for a classroom to decide upon a pet they want and agree to take care of as part of their class's responsibility. Class pets will remain in a child's mind forever!

Here are Some More Ways to Start Bringing More Humor into Your Life and Class

The following sections are adapted from HelpGuide.org, "Laughter is the Best Medicine."

Laughter is a natural part of life that is innate and inborn. Infants begin smiling during the first weeks of life and laugh out loud within months of being born. Even if you did not grow up in a household where laughter was a common sound, you can learn to laugh at any stage of life.

Begin by setting aside special times to seek out humor and laughter, as you might with working out, and build from there. Eventually, you'll want to incorporate humor and laughter into your life, finding it naturally in everything you do. You will feel better, and anyone around you will as well.

Smile, the Action Is Easy and Free

Smiling is the beginning of laughter. *Like laughter, it's contagious.* Pioneers in "laugh therapy" find it's possible to laugh without even experiencing a funny event. The same holds for smiling. When you look at someone or see something even mildly pleasing, practice smiling, it will do wonders for your soul.

Always Count Your Blessings

Literally make a list of those things you are thankful for. The simple act of considering the good things in your life will distance you from negative thoughts that are a barrier to humor and laughter. When you're in a state of sadness, you have further to travel to get to humor and laughter. Sadness can snowball into having a bad day, and you can make the choice to change it.

When You Hear Laughter, Move Toward It

Doing this will surprise you how it can change your present mood, and moving toward the levity, just might change your whole attitude. What do we have to lose, except possibly a bad mood? Sometimes humor and laughter are private, a shared joke among a small group, but usually not. More often, people are very happy to share something funny because it gives them an opportunity to laugh again, and feed off the humor you find in it. When you hear laughter, seek it out and ask, *"What's funny?"*

Spend Time with Fun, Playful People

These are people who laugh easily—both at themselves and at life's absurdities—and who routinely find the humor in everyday events. Their playful point of view and laughter are contagious. Others are drawn to them and are lightened by their levity.

Bring Humor into Conversations

> Just so you know, teachers don't "have the summer off." They just do a year's worth of work in ten months.
>
> —Author unknown, however . . . *any* teacher would say this one!

Ask students or parents, "What's the funniest thing that happened to you today? This week? In your life?" Why did you think it was funny? Did others laugh? Do you think it is OK to laugh at yourself?[9]

Write Down Jokes That Seem Especially Funny to YOU

It is difficult to remember jokes most of the time, or you spoil it by telling the "punch line" before giving all the details. Why not jot them down; say them to family members for practice first. If they find the joke funny, you are good to go and take it to the classroom, if it is appropriate, of course!

How Do You Develop Your Sense of Humor?

First and foremost, *take yourself less seriously*! This important characteristic will help us laugh so much more. We hear this over and over, yet many forget this warning most of the time. We've all known the classic tight-jawed "sourpuss" who takes everything with deathly seriousness and never laughs at anything. Those people are usually not fun to even be around!

There are so many things that are basically funny in life and living, especially when it relates to teaching and school. Use some of the following humorous quotes to "lighten up" your serious times, or your class, or share a few of these often with those who teach or are educators. Some are motivational, and others silly or funny:

Good thoughts cannot ever be ugly. You can have a wonky nose and a crooked mouth and a double chin and stick-out teeth, but if you have good thoughts they will shine out of your face like sunbeams and you will always look lovely.

—Roald Dahl

A police officer came to my house and asked me where I was between five and six.
I replied: Kindergarten.

—Author unknown (Kids love this one, too!)

As you can see, there are so many clever quotes from people everywhere, from different professions, during different times of history; showing men and women alike have a great sense of humor. Wouldn't life be a lot better to see the sunny or "funny side of life"? Here you only read two, but when you get to the appendix of this book, look for so many more to use soon in the home or classroom.

After realizing that laughter and humor, in general, can add so much more joy in living, while helping us to be happier, healthier, and more content with our set of circumstances, why not start using them more? Seeing the glass half full rather than half empty helps in so many ways, as emphasized throughout this book.

Your best teacher is your last mistake!

—Ralph Nader

Hmmm, this last one makes me stop to evaluate what Ralph Nader meant, exactly. He is actually saying that "mistakes are how we learn best" . . . right?

Some events are clearly sad and not occasions for laughter. But most events in life don't carry an overwhelming sense of either sadness or delight. They fall into the "gray zone" of ordinary life, giving you the choice to laugh or not.

End adaptation.

How Laughing Leads to Learning

Research suggests that humor produces psychological and physiological benefits that help students learn. By injecting humor into lessons students will remain more alert and attentive to the lesson on the board. It is important though, that to be effective, comedy must complement—and not distract from—course material.

> In fact, instructors who use distracting or inappropriate humor can actually interfere with students' learning," suggests research by interpersonal communications researcher Melissa Bekelja Wanzer, EdD, of Canisius College.
>
> However, a growing body of research suggests that, when used effectively, classroom comedy can improve student performance by reducing anxiety, boosting participation and increasing students' motivation to focus on the material. Moreover, the benefits might not be limited to students: Research suggests that students rate professors who make learning fun significantly higher than others. [10]

Engaging Students

Students in today's society are overstressed and overstimulated. "Laughter has been shown to stimulate a physiological effect that decreases stress hormones such as serum cortisol, dopac and epinephrine." Students can't become engaged until they are destressed. Using relatable content and humor is a great way to get distracted students engaged in the lesson.

> "Well-planned, appropriate, contextual humor can help students ingrain information," explains Randy Garner, who in his introduction to psychology course uses TV programs like the audition episodes from *American Idol* to demonstrate such psychological concepts as self-handicapping and selection bias. . . . Ohio University-Zanesville psychology professors Mark Shatz, PhD, and Frank LoSchiavo, PhD, found that when they insert self-deprecating jokes, psychology-related cartoons and top 10 lists in an online introductory psychology course, their students more often logged on to the online system Blackboard and were more likely to enjoy the class. [11]

Students are most stressed when they are preparing for an exam or taking an exam. Writing a joke on the board or putting up a funny cartoon can help them relax and focus more.

Drawing the Line between Being Educational and Being Distractive

Communications researcher Jennings Bryant, PhD, of the Institute for Communications Research at the University of Alabama, says you need to focus on the learning first. Bryant has worked as a script consultant for *Sesame Street* and *The Electric Company* and has studied classroom humor. Dr. Bryant and his colleague Dr. Dolf Zillmann "found that although humor can make the learning experience more pleasant, it must be attuned to the audience's knowledge to enhance students' attention, improve the classroom environment or lower students' test anxieties."[12] Meaning, as Bryant explains, if a teacher has too many jokes, the student might miss the message.

> He who laughs most, learns best.
>
> —John Cleese

We see there are many different opinions about using humor in the classroom, and whether or not it is appropriate or even necessary. However, most teachers, children, and adults find that, if used correctly and for the right emphasis, humor embellishes their learning!

PARENTS, STUDENTS, AND EDUCATION CAN CONNECT WITH HUMOR

Parental involvement is very important in a student's academic success. While brainpower, work ethic, and even genetics all play important roles in student achievement, the determining factor comes down to what kind of support system the child has at home. *Adding a "sprinkle of humor" can make that support system so much better and lead to improved learning.*[13]

Here are some amazing facts about parental involvement:

1. "Students with two parents operating in supportive roles are 52 percent more likely to enjoy school and get straight As. . . . The data shows, predictably, that having one parent involved is better than having none at all.[14]

2. "Having a supportive mother makes a slightly more positive difference than having a supportive father. Having a supportive
father, however, leads to slightly higher grades than having a
supportive mother."[15]
3. "Parents with advanced degrees are 3.5 times as likely as parents
without high school degrees to teach their children the alphabet,
2.4 times more likely to teach them to count to 20, 1.8 times as
likely to teach them how to write their first name, and 2.8 times
more likely to read to them daily."[16]
4. "Between 1996 and 2007, the percentage of 'low-income' students typically held back a grade reached 25 percent, while the
percentage of 'non-poor' students remained low and relatively
constant."[17]

Obviously, many financial, economic, and social situations are never an
"easy fix" however hard we want them to be repaired. Therefore, we
should look at those conditions we can change. This book has shown
you how humor and laughter in the home or at school can change how
children learn and retain important information for their lives and ca-
reers. The additional benefits to the parent or teacher using humorous
teaching techniques cannot be ignored.

Let's all discover ways to help our parents, teachers, and children
create the child's best learning environment. Since there is no expense
involved in making "light of life," teaching children with laughter, or
learning how to deal with anger, stress and bullying . . . we realize that
children can thrive even more!

*The following sections are adapted from HelpGuide.org, "Laughter is
the Best Medicine"*

Laugh at Yourself

Share your embarrassing moments. The best way to take yourself less
seriously is to talk about times when you took yourself too seriously. For
instance, say: "You know you're a teacher when you start thinking about
fall activities in the middle of July!"

Attempt to Laugh at Situations Rather Than Whine

Look for the humor in a bad situation, and uncover the irony and absurdity of life. This will help improve your mood and the mood of those around you.

Surround Yourself with Reminders to "Lighten Up"

Keep a toy on your desk or in your car. Put up a funny poster in your office. Choose a computer screensaver that makes you laugh. Frame photos of you and your family or friends having fun. Children love to see pictures of your pets! [18]

Keep Things in Perspective

Many things in life are beyond your control—particularly the behavior of other people. While you might think taking the weight of the world on your shoulders is admirable, in the long run it's unrealistic, unproductive, unhealthy, and even egotistical. [19]

Deal with Your Stress

Stress is a major impediment to humor and laughter.

Pay Attention to Children and Emulate Them

They are the experts on playing, *taking life lightly*, and laughing.

Using Humor and Play to Overcome Challenges and Enhance Your Life

> Football players have the Super Bowl. Runners have the Olympics. Teachers Have "Back to School." Armed with new ideas, fresh views, a stapler, and glue. GAME ON!
>
> —Author unknown

The ability to laugh and have fun with others not only helps you to relax, but it also helps you to connect with people and solve problems. When you "become the problem" and take yourself too seriously, it can be hard to think outside the box and find new solutions. But when you play with the problem, you can often transform it into an opportunity for creative learning. Also on the funnier side . . . when all else fails, you can pray for a fire drill!

Helpguide.org states "As laughter, humor, and play become an integrated part of your life, your creativity will flourish and new discoveries for playing with friends, coworkers, acquaintances, and loved ones will occur to you daily. Humor takes you to a higher place where you can view the world from a more relaxed, positive, creative, joyful, and balanced perspective."[20]

Resources and Books to Help Parents and Teachers

There are so many resources and books available to help parents and teachers discover the ways to use humor in creative, yet successful ways:

How to Make Close Friends: Tips on meeting people and building strong friendships

https://www.helpguide.org/articles/relationships/how-to-make-friends.htm

The Health Benefits of Dogs (and Cats): How caring for pets can help you deal with depression, anxiety, and stress

https://www.helpguide.org/articles/emotional-health/the-health-benefits-of-pets.htm

General Information about Health and Humor

He who laughs most, learns best.

—John Cleese

Articles on Health and Humor: Psychologist and humor-training specialist Paul McGhee offers a series of articles on humor, laughter, and health.

http://www.laughterremedy.com/articles/health_articles.html

Laughter is the "Best Medicine" for Your Heart: Describes a study that found that laughter helps prevent heart disease.

http://www.umm.edu/news-and-events/news-releases/2009/laughter-is-the-best-medicine-for-your-heart

Laughter Therapy: Guide to the healing power of laughter, including the research supporting laughter therapy.

http://www.cancercenter.com/treatments/laughter-therapy/

The Social Benefits of Laughter: Article on the social benefits of laughter and the important role it plays in the relationships between people.

https://www.psychologytoday.com/articles/200304/the-benefits-laughter

The Science of Laughter: Psychologist and laughter researcher Robert Provine, PhD, explains the power of laughter, humor, and play as social tools.

https://www.psychologytoday.com/articles/200011/the-science-laughter

There are so many references available online and in the library, giving all of us information about the health benefits, both socially and emotionally, of humor and laughter. Take the time to do some research, to help you in your more meaningful teaching and in a happier life as well.

> Only Robinson Crusoe had everything done by Friday!
> *End adaptation.*
>
> —Author unknown

BRINGING MORE LAUGHTER AND HUMOR INTO YOUR LIFE AND THE FACULTY ROOM: HUMOR IN THE WORKPLACE

> I teach high school math. I sell a product to a market that doesn't want it, but is forced by law to buy it.
>
> —Dan Meyer

There are a series of articles on using humor in the workplace to reduce job stress, improve morale, boost productivity and creativity, and improve communication. The funny stories below are "old-time humor" you can use on your fellow teachers and to show children in your classes how easy they have it today! Naturally, all humor needs to be used at the proper developmental level of the student and be appropriate.

> *Someone asked the other day, "What was your favorite fast food when you were growing up?"*

"We didn't have fast food when I was growing up," I informed him.

"All the food was slow."

"C'mon, seriously. Where did you eat?"

"It was a place called 'at home,'" I explained.

"Mom cooked every day and when Dad got home from work, we sat down together at the dining room table, and if I didn't like what she put on my plate I was allowed to sit there until I did like it."

By this time, the kid was laughing so hard I was afraid he was going to suffer serious internal damage, so I didn't tell him the part about how I had to have permission to leave the table. But here are some other things I would have told him about my childhood, if I figured his system could have handled it:

Some parents never owned their own house, never wore Levis, never set foot on a golf course, never traveled out of the country or had a credit card.

In their later years they had something called a revolving charge card. The card was good only at Sears Roebuck. Or maybe it was Sears & Roebuck.

Either way, there is no Roebuck anymore. Maybe he died?

My parents never drove me to soccer practice. This was mostly because we never had heard of soccer. I had a bicycle that weighed probably fifty pounds, and only had one speed, slow. We didn't have a television in our house until I was nineteen. It was, of course, black and white, and the station went off the air at midnight, after playing the national anthem and a poem about God; it came back on the air at about 6 a.m. And there was usually a locally produced news and farm show on, featuring local people.

I was twenty-one before I tasted my first pizza, it was called "pizza pie."

When I bit into it, I burned the roof of my mouth and the cheese slid off, swung down, plastered itself against my chin and burned that, too. It's still the best pizza I ever had.

I never had a telephone in my room. The only phone in the house was in the living room and it was on a party line. Before you could dial, you had to listen and make sure some people you didn't know weren't already using the line.

Pizzas were not delivered to our home, but milk was. All newspapers were delivered by boys and all boys delivered newspapers— my brother delivered a newspaper, six days a week. It cost seven *cents a paper, of which he got to keep two cents. He had to get up at 6 a.m. every morning.*

On Saturday, he had to collect the forty-two cents from his customers. His favorite customers were the ones who gave him fifty cents and told him to keep the change. His least favorite customers were the ones who seemed to never be home on collection day.

Movie stars kissed with their mouths shut. At least, they did in the movies. There were no movie ratings because all movies were responsibly produced for everyone to enjoy viewing, without profanity or violence or most anything offensive.

If you grew up in a generation before there was fast food, you may want to share some of these memories with your children or grandchildren. Just don't blame me if they do not believe you, or die laughing! Growing up isn't what it used to be, is it? And try to remember how things were when you grew up. (Author unknown)

Memories of Youth Long Ago

My Dad is cleaning out my grandmother's house and he brought me an old Royal Crown Cola bottle. In the bottle top was a stopper with a bunch of holes in it. I knew immediately what it was, but my daughter had no idea. She thought they had tried to make it a salt shaker or something. I knew it as the bottle that sat on the end of the ironing board to "sprinkle" clothes with because we didn't have steam irons. Man, I am old! (Author unknown)

How Many Do You Remember?

1. Headlight dimmer switches on the floor.
2. Ignition switches on the dashboard.
3. Heaters mounted on the inside of the fire wall.
4. Real iceboxes.
5. Pant leg clips for bicycles without chain guards.
6. Soldering irons you heat on a gas burner.
7. Using hand signals for cars without turn signals. (Author unknown)

Older Than Dirt Quiz

Here is a quote from a comedian from long ago. You may or may not want to use this one:

In the school I went to, they asked a kid to prove the law of gravity
and he threw the teacher out of the window.

—Rodney Dangerfield

Count all the ones that you remember, not the ones you were told
about! (Ratings at the bottom.)

1. Blackjack chewing gum
2. Wax Coke-shaped bottles with colored sugar water
3. Candy cigarettes
4. Soda pop machines that dispensed glass bottles
5. Coffee shops or diners with tableside juke boxes
6. Home milk delivery in glass bottles with cardboard stoppers
7. Party lines on the telephone
8. Newsreels before the movie
9. P.F. Flyers
10. Butch wax
11. TV test patterns that came on at night after the last show and
    were there until TV shows started again in the morning. (There
    were only three channels . . . [if you were fortunate])
12. Peashooters
13. Howdy Doody
14. 45 RPM records
15. S & H Greenstamps
16. Hi-fis
17. Metal ice trays with lever
18. Mimeograph paper
19. Blue flashbulb
20. Packards
21. Roller skate keys
22. Cork popguns
23. Drive-ins
24. Studebakers
25. Washtub wringers

Key:

If you remembered 0–5 = You're still young
If you remembered 6–10 = You are getting older

If you remembered 11–15 = Don't tell your age

If you remembered 16–25 = You're older than dirt! And this score includes the author![21]

This author might be "older than dirt" but those memories are some of the best parts of my life.

Sometimes it is important for us as adults to remember from long ago, with a giggle, to see how much humor there is just in our old-fashioned inventions and ways of living. By doing this silly exercise, you can see why it is so important to use humor in your teaching and dealing with children. It demonstrates how humor can make you feel good and relax a little at the same time! Try to lighten up, be committed to using more humor . . . enjoy a little levity in your classroom, and you will reap the benefits of children listening better and loving you even more than they already do!

Commitment Matters

Quote of the day:

> Put your mind to it. And while you're at it, put your fingers, toes, arms, legs, eyes, mouth, and heart into it.
>
> —Ralph Marston

NOTES

1. Lawrence Robinson, Melinda Smith, and Jeanne Segal, "Laughter Is the Best Medicine," HelpGuide.org, https://www.helpguide.org/articles/mental-health/laughter-is-the-best-medicine.htm#social. Used with permission.

2. Ibid.

3. Ibid.

4. "Developing a Sense of Humor," What to Expect, 2015, https://www.whattoexpect.com/toddler/toddler-growth-and-development/developing-a-sense-of-humor.aspx.

5. Ibid.

6. Ibid.

7. Robinson, Smith, and Segal, "Laughter Is the Best Medicine."

8. Lawrence Robinson and Jeanne Segal, "Mood-Boosting Power of Dogs," HelpGuide.org, https://www.helpguide.org/articles/mental-health/mood-boosting-power-of-dogs.htm.

9. Robinson, Smith, and Segal, "Laughter Is the Best Medicine."

10. Zak Stambor, "How Laughing Leads to Learning," *American Psychological Association*, 37, no. 6. (June 2006), http://www.apa.org/monitor/jun06/learning.aspx.

11. Ibid.

12. Ibid.

13. Ronald A. Berk, *Humor as an Instructional Defibrillator*

14. Andrianes Pinantoan, InformEd blog, "The Effect of Parental Involvement in School and Education," June 25, 2013, http://www.opencolleges.edu.au/informed/features/the-effect-of-parental-involvement-in-academic-achievement/.

15. Ibid.

16. Ibid.

17. Ibid.

18. Robinson, Smith, and Segal, "Laughter Is the Best Medicine."

19. Lawrence Robinson, Melinda Smith, and Jeanne Segal, "Stress Management: Using Self-Help Techniques for Dealing with Stress," Helpguide.org International, https://www.helpguide.org/articles/stress/stress-management.htm.

20. Robinson, Smith, and Segal, "Laughter Is the Best Medicine."

21. Lawrence Robinson, Melinda Smith, and Jeanne Segal, "How to Bring More Laughter into Your Life," Helpguide.org International, https://www.helpguide.org/articles/emotional-health/laughter-is-the-best-medicine.htm.

7

CONCLUSION

With mirth and laughter let old wrinkles come.

—William Shakespeare

It is obvious that humor and laughter make children happy! (Adults too!) They want to learn more, listen more, and retain what they have learned *if the lessons are presented in a fun and meaningful way* to them. Funny poems, stories, chants, or songs that can be about skills in reading, writing, science, math, social studies, or cultural arts . . . will be *retained and retold* for years to come.

Former students whom this author has run into as high-school students and even adults still can remember things we learned in second grade and even Kindergarten! Not just the silly school songs, *but the mandated skills* taught through poems, songs, chants, games, and so on. This is a "true test of retention" passed with flying colors, this passionate teacher believes.

As pointed out throughout this book, "Laughter, some say . . . it's the best medicine in the world." *This author would tend to agree.*

So start smiling and laughing as much as you possibly can. We have already learned how it can actually improve your health. Besides strengthening your immune system, it boosts mood, diminishes pain, and protects you from the damaging effects of stress. We all can attest to how humor *can brighten up your day*, not to mention the importance of adding years to your life.

A study in Norway found that people with a strong sense of humor outlived those who don't laugh as much. The difference was particularly notable for those battling cancer.[1]

The fabulous work that the late Danny Thomas, his daughter Marlo Thomas, and her family have done extremely graciously, for so many years, is truly an "amazing grace!" St. Jude Children's Research Hospital has been helping children and their families to survive cancer, or at the very least to enjoy the time they have left on this earth. And with not one penny paid by the family, it boggles the mind how they can support such a huge research/care hospital! Their short and poignant motto is "Finding cures. Saving children."

> *Laughter is important*, not only because it makes us happy, it also has actual health benefits. And that's because laughter completely engages the body and releases the mind. It connects us to others, and that in itself has a healing effect.
>
> —Marlo Thomas

In case you are not familiar with this stellar organization, here is a quote:

> The Danny Thomas–St. Jude Society is named for the hospital's beloved founder, Danny Thomas. Danny's devotion to saving children with cancer and other life-threatening diseases lives on through the legacy of our society members, whose remarkable gifts help to ensure that St. Jude can continue its cutting-edge research and unsurpassed patient care. Most importantly, society members help to ensure that families *never receive a bill* from St. Jude for treatment, travel, housing or food—because all a family should worry about is helping their child live.[2]

When Danny Thomas, Marlo's father, founded St. Jude more than fifty years ago, he believed we could change the fate of children battling deadly diseases like cancer, and a huge part of their staff's protocol is using humor and laughter daily to cheer up anyone who might need it.

Humor has so much power to *renew and heal*. The ability to laugh easily and frequently is a valuable resource for surmounting problems. Laughter can enhance your relationships and *support both physical and emotional health*.[3]

I will follow the upward road today; I will keep my face to the light. I will think high thoughts as I go my way; I will do what I know is right. I will look for the flowers by the side of the road; *I will laugh and love and be strong.* I will try to lighten another's load this day as I fare along.

—Mary S. Edgar

Laughter is the sun that drives winter from the human face.

—Victor Hugo

If we're destroying our trees and destroying our environment and hurting animals and hurting one another and all that stuff, there's got to be a very powerful energy to fight that. I think we need more love in the world. We need more kindness, more compassion, more joy, more laughter. I definitely want to contribute to that.

—Ellen DeGeneres

I hope you will go out and let stories happen to you, and that you will work them, water them with your blood and tears and your laughter till they bloom, till you yourself burst into bloom.

—Clarissa Pinkola Estes

You can't deny laughter; when it comes, it plops down in your favorite chair and stays as long as it wants.

—Stephen King

Are you also wondering now what you can do *outside of school*? Why not share more funny moments, even if they are embarrassing, with friends and family? To learn to *laugh at yourself* is a huge accomplishment, and one that will make others share their funniest blunders, too.

The person who can bring the *spirit of laughter* into a room is indeed blessed.

—Bennett Cerf

Close friends contribute to our personal growth. They also contribute to our personal pleasure, making the music sound sweeter, the wine taste richer, *the laughter ring louder* because they are there.
—Judith Viorst

You might host a "game night" for friends, like the dice game Bunco. This game makes everyone talk, giggle, and laugh. Players move from table to table and get to know the entire group. It is easy to learn, and fun for all ages.

> I believe that laughter is the best *emotional Band-Aid* ® in the world. It's like nature's Neosporin®.
>
> —Matt LeBlanc

> I feel now it's useless to keep hoping. The way things are today, we live in a *world that needs laughter*, and I've decided if I can make people laugh, I'm making a more important contribution.
>
> —Paul Lynde

Make sure you *seek out more playful people* in your life that laugh easily. Who wants to be around a "Debbie Downer"? Positive, cheerful people can add more joy to your life, and maybe *show you* how to do the same for others. Always move toward laughter, when you hear it.

This next short quote says it all, doesn't it?

> He (or she) who laughs, *lasts!*
>
> —Mary Pettibone Poole

Have a hearty laugh over every amusing situation that comes your way. Laugh especially *at yourself* and smile at the simplest pleasures in your daily routines. Otherwise your life can become quite humdrum! Who wants that? Not you, your children, your students, or even your parent volunteers.

CLASSROOM MANAGEMENT CAN BE FUN!

With smiles and laughter, your days will become lighter, more joyous, and more bearable even on those days when nothing seems to go as you had planned. We all have had some days, that we now wonder how we even "survived" it all. But fortunately, with a little levity, those horrid days can seem not so bad. Besides, your smiling face looks much more appealing and beautiful when allowed to turn a frown upside down. So what if a few distinguished wrinkles are added in the joy of giving and receiving humor?

Our teachers are one of our *most valuable resources today*, and the stress some of them face can be almost unbearable! With the physical health benefits of laughter like boosting immunity, lowering stress hormones, decreasing pain, and preventing heart disease, there is more hope for them through laughter. Relaxing muscles is an added benefit. These physical benefits can certainly help children as well!

If only our children, parents, teachers, and people of the world could believe the following quote by Germany Kent, how much better off the universe could become. Children would feel great about themselves with positive self-esteem. Parents could relax more about their jobs as parents, and teachers could do the same about teaching their best lessons ever.

All would learn to create, love, laugh, and live healthier and better lives. The peoples of the world would do the same making our universe a peaceful place for everyone. And because of doing these positive things, we all would be doing great things for everyone!

> You're going to make it; You're going to be at peace; You're going to create, and love, and laugh, and live; You're going to do great things.
> —Germany Kent

Many of us have had difficult times on our "journey of life," but since we only have the one life to live, why not try our best to enjoy our short time on earth?

> Life is difficult and those who make us laugh are *angels*.
> —Wayne Gerard Trotman

> Comedy is not the opposite of darkness, but its natural bedfellow. Pain makes laughter necessary; *laughter makes pain tolerable*.
> —Mindy Greenstein

> I love to laugh. *Specially at myself.* Sometimes I spend hours doing it.
> —Nuno Roque

No teacher or parent relishes arguments, anger, or disagreements, whether those occur with children or adults:

Laughter and tears are both responses to frustration and exhaustion. I myself prefer to laugh, since there is less cleaning up to do afterward.

—Kurt Vonnegut

Holding on to anger, resentment, and hurt only gives you tense muscles, a headache, and a sore jaw from clenching your teeth. Forgiveness gives you back the laughter and the lightness in your life.

—Joan Lunden

In the sweetness of friendship let there be laughter, and sharing of pleasures. For in the dew of little things the heart finds its morning and is refreshed.

—Khalil Gibran

Give away your smiles to all, *especially children*, freely and in abundance. Spread your laughter around; as many of us already have seen . . . *that laughter IS contagious*! Besides, think of all those you will uplift and perhaps even change their day.

At home or in the classroom, *humor can work miracles* with you as well as the children. Give levity a try. The use of laughter brings down walls and makes you more approachable and trusted. There is no better way to gain the support of your students and their parents.

I think laughter is the best medicine. If you can't laugh at yourself, then you can't laugh at life and the silliness of it all.

—David Hasselhoff

Laughter is one of the very privileges of reason, being confined to the human species.

—Thomas Carlyle

A sense of humor . . . is needed armor. Joy in one's heart and some laughter on one's lips is a sign that the person down deep has a pretty good grasp of life.

—Hugh Sidey

And to think how other famous people view humor and laughter, show its importance:

The Human Race has one really *effective weapon*, and that is laughter!

—Mark Twain

A day without laughter is a day wasted!

—Charlie Chaplin

The most wasted of all days is one *without* laughter.

—E. E. Cummings

HOW TO HAVE A SUCCESSFUL NEW YEAR

Often as teachers, we worry about how parents will perceive us, or understand our relationship with their child, and whether they see value in our strategies or lessons taught.

Obtaining the parents' approval and support is key to a successful year, as any teacher knows!

You might find out that nothing balances your nervous system faster than communicating face-to-face with another person. Add laughter to that communication and you have a *powerful antidote* to stress, pain, anxiety, and conflict.

Humor inspires hopes, connects you to others, lightens your burdens, and can keep you grounded, focused, and alert! (Why wouldn't that be true with children?) Laughter can also help you to release anger and be more forgiving.

I was irrevocably betrothed to laughter, the sound of which has always seemed to me to be the most civilized music in the world.

—Peter Ustinov

If laughter cannot solve your problems, it will definitely *dissolve* your problems; so that you can think clearly *what to do* about them.

—Dr. Madan Kataria

The "bridge to the parents' trust" is through their *own child*. What the child brings home from the teacher on paper is important if it is done in a caring, yet humorous way. More importantly, however, is what info is also demonstrated by their child . . . his or her remembering *facts of importance* through poems, stories, songs, chants, and so on. Now the parent *sees and hears* that their child is not only enjoying the classroom and teacher, but is *additionally retaining the skills taught*.

When this "magical connection" happens, you will be amazed how much help you can get from volunteers! Often you hardly have to ask, since human nature is to support what we believe is best. For parents that means support for their child and the entire classroom. Many parents will then *want to* participate in "sharing" culturally, cooking, or helping with learning stations.

Others will feel more comfortable behind the scenes, saving you hours, by prepping materials or collating books for the entire class. Even the dreaded jobs of carnival or party organization get taken care of easily. Hard to believe, you may be thinking?

Just give humor a chance:

> Hearty laughter is a good way to *jog internally* without having to go outdoors.
>
> —Norman Cousins

> Laughter is the *closest distance* between two people.
>
> —Victor Borge

BETTER RETENTION FOR STUDENTS IS PARAMOUNT

> *I believe that imagination is stronger than knowledge*. That myth is more potent than history. That dreams are more powerful than facts. That hope always triumphs over experience. That *laughter is the only cure for grief*. And I believe that love is stronger than death.
>
> —Robert Fulghum

E. B. White famously stated, "Humor can be dissected, as a frog can, but the thing dies in the process." At the risk of committing some sort of "humorcide," a type of scientific dissection must take place if teachers are to consider harnessing the powerful effects of humor, not only to increase joy and enhance the classroom environment, but also to *improve learner outcomes*.

Teachers understand that humor is *naturally social*. How many times have you heard that same dumb knock-knock joke spread through your classroom? The contagious nature of humor naturally builds a *sense of community* by lowering defenses and bringing individuals together. If the brain is faced with an inconsistency, then laughter is the response when it is resolved in an unexpected way. This sentence, "Memorization is what we resort to when what we are *learning makes no sense*," may make us smile as our brains resolve its inconsistency.

Basically, humor activates our "sense of wonder," which is where learning begins, so it seems logical that humor could enhance retention. A Pew Research poll showed that viewers of humorous news shows such as *The Daily Show* and *The Colbert Report* exhibited *higher retention of news* facts than those who got their news from newspapers, CNN, Fox News, or network stations. When Stephen Colbert demands, "If we don't cut expensive things like Head Start, child nutrition programs, and teachers, what sort of future are we leaving for our children?" viewers laugh . . . and also retain the knowledge of that specific budget issue. [4]

Many studies explain *why we remember things* that make us laugh, such as our favorite songs, poems, stories, and chants learned in our youth, or the details of that funny movie we saw last weekend. This learning that is also fun, can be such an important tool for a teacher! We all want our students to like school, love us, feel success, and retain what is taught . . . don't we? *So why not use this invaluable tool more in our classrooms to teach necessary skills?*

Neuroscience research reveals that humor systematically activates the brain's dopamine reward system, and cognitive studies show that dopamine is important for both goal-oriented motivation and long-term memory, while educational research indicates that correctly-used humor can be an effective intervention to improve retention in students from kindergarten through college. [5]

Well, maybe you have learned some valuable information about the importance of humor for all of us? We hope you will agree that laughter and levity are *"Magical"* . . . not only in classroom management, but as the best way to *"speak a child's language."*

We certainly hope so!

In conclusion, please keep enjoying the quotes throughout this book with smiles and sometimes laughter, or even belly laughs! Go back and reread them over and over to see *their value*, whether the author of the quote is a celebrity, philosopher of long ago, an older person, or even a child.

More importantly,

> If you don't learn to laugh at trouble, you won't have anything to laugh at when you're *old*.
>
> —Edgar Watson Howe

And lastly, there is *much wisdom* in a seemingly simple quote. The following from a well-known "circus man" is one we need to all think about *for the benefit* of our students and children:

> To me there is no picture so beautiful as smiling, bright-eyed, happy children; no music so sweet as their clear and ringing laughter.
>
> —P. T. Barnum

NOTES

1. Laughter is the Best Medicine—The Health Benefits of Humor and Laughter," retrieved 8/25/2017, www.lupuscanada.com

2. St. Jude Society pamphlet, Danny Thomas, founder of St. Jude Cancer Research Hospital for Children, 2015.

3. Helpguide.org "Laughter is the Best Medicine."

4. Sarah Henderson, "Laughter and Learning: Humor Boosts Retention," *Teacher Strategies*, March 31, 2015, George Lucas Educational Foundation, https://www.edutopia.org/blog/laughter-learning-humor-boosts-retention-sarah-henderson

5. Ibid.

APPENDIX

There are so many *wonderful quotes* of people from all walks of life; some are no longer living, while others are still around to amaze us with their wisdom. When time, Google their name, if you have never heard of them. Read each one of these quotes slowly . . . and think *how* they pertain to education, daily living, and in using our brains to the fullest!

GREAT QUOTES FOR KIDS ABOUT EDUCATION AND LEARNING

"Even the *wisest mind* has something yet to learn." ~ George Santayana

"Anyone who *stops learning* is old, whether at twenty or eighty. Anyone who keeps learning stays *young.*" ~ Henry Ford

"The *important thing* is not to stop questioning." ~ Albert Einstein

"Learning is a *treasure* that will follow its owner everywhere." ~ Chinese proverb

"None of us is as smart as *all* of us." ~ Ken Blanchard

"A house is not a home unless it contains food and fire *for the mind* as well as the body." ~ Benjamin Franklin

"The *mind* is not a vessel to be filled, but a *fire* to be kindled." ~ Plutarch

"Educating the mind without educating the *heart* is no education at all." ~ Aristotle

"You can tell whether a man is *clever* by his answers. You can tell whether a man is *wise* by his questions." ~ Naguib Mahfouz

"Education is *not* the filling of a pail, but the lighting of a *fire.*" ~ W. B. Yeats

"If you *can't* explain it simply, you don't understand it well enough." ~ Albert Einstein

"Nothing in life is to be feared. It is only to be *understood.*" ~ Marie Curie

"A *mistake* is a crash-course in learning." ~ Billy Anderson

"We are not what we *know* but what we are willing to learn." ~ Mary Catherine Bateson

"He who opens a school door, *closes a prison.*" ~ Victor Hugo

"*Knowledge* will bring you the opportunity to make a difference." ~ Claire Fagan

"*If you change the way you look at things, the things you look at change.*" ~ Wayne Dyer

"*Education* is teaching our children to desire the right things." ~ Plato

"*I believe that we learn by practice.* Whether it means to learn to dance by practicing dancing or to learn to live by practicing living, the principles are the same. Practice means to perform, over and over again . . . in the face of all obstacles, some act of vision, of faith, of desire. Practice is a means of *inviting the perfection* desired." ~ Martha Graham

"*Education is the power* to think clearly, the power to act well in the world's work, and the power to appreciate life." ~ Brigham Young

"I received the fundamentals of my education in school, but that was *not* enough. My real education, the superstructure, the details, the true architecture, I got out of the public *library.* For an impoverished child, whose family could not afford to buy books, the library was the open door to wonder and achievement, and I can never be sufficiently grateful that I had the wit to charge through that door and make the most of it." ~ Isaac Asimov

"Painful as it may be, a significant emotional event can be the catalyst for choosing a direction that serves us—and those around us—more effectively. *Look for the learning.*" ~ Louisa May Alcott

"*Imagination is more important than knowledge.* For knowledge is limited to all we now know and understand, while imagination embraces the entire world, and all there ever will be to know and understand." ~ Albert Einstein

"Life is *not* about how fast you run or how high you climb but how well you *bounce*." ~ Vivian Komori

GENERAL INFORMATION ABOUT HEALTH AND HUMOR

Articles on Health and Humor—Psychologist and humor-training specialist Paul McGhee offers a series of articles on humor, laughter, and health. (Laughter Remedy)

Laughter as Medicine

Laughter is the "Best Medicine" for Your Heart – Describes a study that found that laughter helps prevent heart disease. (University of Maryland Medical Center)

Laughter Therapy – Guide to the healing power of laughter, including the research supporting laughter therapy. (Cancer Treatment Centers of America)

Laugh lots, live longer – Details Norwegian study that found having a strong sense of humor may extend life expectancy. (Scientific American Mind)

Laughter-Based Exercise Program for Older Adults has Health Benefits – Research that shows the health benefits of simulated laughter. (Georgia State University)

No joke: Study finds laughing can burn calories – Outlines a small study that found laughing raises energy expenditure and increases heart rate enough to burn a small amount of calories. (Vanderbilt University Medical Center)

The Social Benefits of Laughter

The Benefits of Laughter – Article on the social benefits of laughter and the important role it plays in the relationships between people. (*Psychology Today*)

The Science of Laughter – Psychologist and laughter researcher Robert Provine, PhD, explains the power of laughter, humor, and play as social tools. (*Psychology Today*)

Bringing More Laughter into Your Life

Humor in the Workplace – Series of articles on using humor in the workplace to reduce job stress, improve morale, boost productivity and creativity, and improve communication. (Laughter Remedy)

So . . . now that you have a true list of excellent and varied resources, you will *not have any excuses* for why you cannot have *more humor* in the classroom and in your life!

Since studies have shown that *children love to learn through jingles, chants and rhymes;* why not teach the following, or better yet, let the class make up their own as a group? Eventually, you will want them to write them down and illustrate in a notebook. Parents love visuals of *what* their child is doing at school, and the booklet serves as a great resource over weekends, school vacations and in the summer, too!

> If Plan A didn't work, don't worry, the alphabet has 25 more letters.
> —Heidi McDonald

Next, we will list some other varieties of jokes, that are *not as educational*, but are quite humorous. *Both types* have their purpose, most would agree. Sometimes the funny ones get more attention, and children love hearing them when they are learning something new!

FUNNY ALPHABET AND LETTER SOUND JINGLES (ALSO TONGUE TWISTERS!)

Our class made up some of the following *Silly Sound Jingles:*

1. **Abraham Ape** Ate Acorns in April and August in Alabama, Arkansas, Austria, Australia and Africa (long and short a)
2. **Bobby Blue Bug** Bent Backwards Badly on Beautiful Brown and Black Blankets in Brazil and Baltimore
3. **Casey Cool Cat** Can Cooperate Carefully with Cards and Candy in Colorado and Canada
4. **Devin Duck** Dunks Doughnuts Delightfully During December in Delaware and Denmark
5. **Emanuel Easter-bunny** Eats Easter Eggs Every Easter in England in Europe (Long and Short E)
6. **Frankie Frog** Feels Funny on Fridays during February in Florida, Finland and France
7. **Gracie Goose** Gave Goofy Green Gifts to Girls in Germany and Georgia
8. **Henry Happy Horse** Has Hay for Hippos and Hyenas in Holland and in Heaven
9. **Ivy Iguana** Introduces Icy Ice-cream in Indiana, Iceland, Ireland, Italy and India (Long and Short Ii)
10. **Jimmy Jaguar** Jumps Jell-O in January, June, and July in Japan and Jeruselum
11. **Kind Katy Kangaroo** Keeps Kites for Kittens in Kenya and Kentucky
12. **Larry Lion** Licks Lovely Lemon Lollipops in Louisiana and Las Vegas
13. **Mike Monkey** Makes Mucho Money on Mondays in March and May in Montana and Mexico
14. **Nancy Newt** Never Needs New Needles Now during November in Norway, New Zealand, New York, or Nevada . . . Nice?
15. **Oliver Octopus** Often Opens Orange Ocean Objects during October in Oregon and Ontario (long and short o)
16. **Paula Pretty Penguin** Pops Purple and Pink Popcorn Politely in Pennsylvania and Poland
17. **Queen Quintana** Quilts Quickly and Quietly for Quarters in Queensland
18. **Richard Rooster** Ran Races by the Red Rogue River in Russia and Romania

19. **Sammy Silver Snake** Sips Several Sodas on Saturday and Sunday on September in Sweden, Switzerland, Scotland, Spain, and South America

20. **Tommy Turtle** Takes Twelve Tacos, Tamales, and Tostadas on Tuesday to Turkey and Texas

21. **Ulysses Unicorn** Uses Ukuleles Usefully in Utah and the Ukraine

22. **Victorious Valerie** Votes for Velvet Valentines on Valentine's Day in Virginia and Victoria

23. **Wanda Witch** Wants White Watermelon on Wednesday for Whales in Washington and West Virginia

24. **Xavier X-man** X-rays X-kids and X-moms externally

25. **Yolanda Yellow Yak** Yells . . . "Yikes!" and "Yes!" in the Yukon and in Yellowstone Park.

26. **Zelda Zebra** Zips Zippers Zealously in Zealand or at the Zoo.

(Of course, you might need to make up *shorter ones* for the very young. Some of these longer examples would be fine even in high school, having students giggle while finding the places on the map or globe! *Why not have a Geography lesson at the same time?* Two skills for the price of one!)

Another fun activity is having your children add cities, states, countries, and continents to the above list. This will build their *alphabetizing skills,* yet enjoying what they are doing during the task! Have students work in pairs or groups to make up the longest, "correct" list.

Then let group leaders read what they came up with as a sharing and learning activity. *Always remember to challenge your students, with meaningful, yet entertaining activities!*

Now let's get onto the *"sillier stuff"* that kids eat up!

TEACHER/CHILD JOKES

20 Funny Knock, Knock Jokes for Kids

- Knock, knock. Who's there? Canoe! Canoe who? *Canoe come out and play with me today?*

- Knock, knock. Who's there? Who! Who who? *That's what an owl says!*
- Knock, knock. Who's there? Lettuce. Lettuce who? *Lettuce in, it's cold out here.*
- Knock, knock. Who's there? Honey bee. Honey bee who? *Honey bee a dear and get me some juice.*
- Knock, knock. Who's there? Wooden shoe. Wooden shoe who? *Wooden shoe like to hear another joke?*
- Knock, knock. Who's there? A broken pencil. A broken pencil who? *Oh, never mind it's pointless.*
- Knock, knock. Who's there? Cow says. Cow says who? *No silly, a cow says Mooooo!*
- Knock, knock. Who's there? Double. Double who? *W!*
- Knock, knock. Who's there? Mikey! Mikey who? *Mikey doesn't fit in the keyhole!*
- Knock, knock. Who's there? Atch. Atch who? *Bless you!*
- Knock, knock. Who's there? I am. I am who? *You don't know who you are?*
- Knock, knock. Who's there? Ya. Ya Who? *Wow, I'm excited to see you too.*
- Knock, knock. Who's there? Figs. Figs who? *Figs the doorbell, it's broken!*
- Knock, knock. Who's there? Boo! Boo who? *Don't cry, it's just me.*
- Knock, knock. Who's there? Iva. Iva who? *I've a sore hand from knocking!*
- Knock, knock. Who's there? A little old lady. A little old lady who? *I didn't know you could yodel.*
- Will you remember me in 2 minutes? Yes. Knock, knock. Who's there? *Hey, you didn't remember me!*
- Knock, knock. Who's there? Banana. Banana who? Knock, knock. Who's there? Banana. Banana who? Knock, knock. Who's there? Banana. Banana who? Knock, knock. Who's there? Orange. Orange who? *Orange you glad I didn't say banana?*
- Knock knock, who's there? Europe, Europe who? *You're a poo, and very rude, too!*

source: *http://www.jokes4us.com/animaljokes/dinosaurjokes.html*

DINOSAUR JOKES

What child does not find fascination with dinosaurs??? Not all of these are tremendously clever to us, but many will make children giggle and love you for telling a joke *before* starting a new lesson. Such an *easy way* to win over good listeners!

- Q: Why can't you hear a pterodactyl using the bathroom? A: *Because the 'p' is silent*
- Q: What do you call it when a dinosaur gets in a car accident? A: *Tyrannosaurus wreck!*
- Q: What do you call a dinosaur with an extensive vocabulary? A: *A Thesaurus.*
- Q: What do dinosaurs have that no other animals have? A: *Baby Dinosaurs.*
- Q: How do you ask a dinosaur to lunch? A: *Tea Rex?*
- Q: What do you call a T-Rex that gets into a fight with the Indominus Rex? A: *Dino-sore.*
- Q: What did the female dinosaur call her blouse making business? A: *Try Sara's Tops*
- Q: Why are dinosaurs no longer around? A: *Because their eggs stink.*
- Q: Who makes dinosaur clothes? A: *Dino-sewer.*
- Q: Why did the dinosaur cross the road? A: *The chicken hadn't evolved yet!*
- Q: Which dinosaur can't stay out of the rain? A: *A Stegosaur-rust*
- Q: What do you get if you cross a pig with a dinosaur? A: *Jurassic Pork!*
- Q. What do you call a dinosaur as tall as a house, with long sharp teeth, 12 claws on each foot and a personal stereo over his ears? A. *Anything you like; he won't hear you!*
- Q. How do you know if there is a Brachiosaurus in bed with you? A. *By the Dinosnores.*
- Q: Where does a Tyrannosaurus sit when he comes to stay? A: *Anywhere he wants to.*
- Q: What do you call a dinosaur that's a noisy sleeper? A: *A Brontosnorus.*
- Q: Why are there old dinosaur bones in the museum? A: *Because they can't afford new ones!*

Q: Why did the dinosaur cross the road? A: *Because the chicken joke wasn't invented yet.*

Q: What do you call a dinosaur that eats its vegetables? A: *A Broci-leasoarus*

Q: Can you name 10 dinosaurs in 10 seconds? A: *Yes, 8 Iguanadons and 2 Stegasaurus.*

Q: What do you call a dinosaur with a foul mouth? A: *Bronto-swore-us.*

Q: Which dinosaur slept all day? A: *The Dino-snore!*

source: *http://www.jokes4us.com/animaljokes/dinosaurjokes.html*

You might be saying that your eyes are starting to glaze over from *"Dino sore eye us."* Yes, this one is very bad . . . but many silly students will even think that is sort of funny!

ANIMAL JOKES

We cannot leave out those children who are *not* wild about dinosaurs, and maybe prefer jokes about *animals* in general. Here a few you can use to get their attention when beginning a new lesson. Even better, write one on the board as they read the question; then ask who knows the answer. All children like to *give their own guess*, and it piques the entire class's interest.

Q: Why don't they play poker in the jungle? A: *Too many cheetahs.*

Q: What is the difference between a cat and a comma? A: *One has the paws before the claws and the other has the clause before the pause.*

Q: Where do dogs go when they lose their tails? A: *To the retail store.*

Q: What kind of dog tells time? A: *A watch dog.*

Q: What has four legs and an arm? A: *A happy pit bull.*

Q: Why is a tree like a dog? A: *Because they both lose their bark when they die.*

Q: Did you hear about the cowboy who got himself a dachshund? A: *Everyone kept telling him to get a long, little doggie.*

Q: Did you hear about the new breed in pet shops? A: *They crossed a pit bull with a collie; it bites your leg off and goes for help.*

Q: How do you know if there is an elephant under the bed? A: *Your nose is touching the ceiling.*

Q: Why did the turtle cross the road? A: *To get to the Shell station!*

Q: Why did chicken Jim Morrison cross the road? A: *To break on through to the other side.*

Q: Why do birds fly South? A: *Because it's too far to walk.*

Q: Why do hummingbirds hum? A: *Because they don't know the words.*

Q: Where does a blackbird go for a drink? A: *To a crow bar.*

Q: Why was the crow perched on a telephone wire? A: *He was going to make a long-distance caw.*

Q: What did the chick say when it saw an orange in the nest? A: *Look at the orange mama laid. (We don't get it either!) Oh, Orange Marmalade!*

Q: Is it good manners to eat fried chicken with your fingers? A: *No, you should eat your fingers separately.*

Q: Why do hens lay eggs? A: *If they dropped them, they'd break.*

Q: Why do seagulls live near the sea? A: *Because if they lived near the bay, they would be called bagels.*

Q: Diner: Do you serve chicken here? A: *Waiter: Sit down, sir. We serve anyone.*

Q: Diner: I can't eat this chicken. Call the manager. A: *Waiter: It's no use. He can't eat it either.*

Q: Which side of a chicken has the most feathers? A: *The outside.*

Q: What do you get when you cross a parrot with a centipede? A: *A walkie-talkie, of course.*

Q: Why did the farmer name his pig "ink"? A: *Because he kept running out of his pen (took us a while, too)*

Well, there are plenty of jokes for a few lessons, but there are many *other ways* to involve humor in your teaching. Jokes are just very quick to do, easy to remember and children relate well to them. Why not put one of those jokes, or questions and answers up *on the board each morning* for the class to copy in a notebook each morning, while you do the roll sheet, and morning tasks of lunch count, etc?

Then you can take their "guesses" later, and finally give the answer for them to write their answers next to the question in their notebook. This is a great way to keep them busy, very entertained, brains stimulated and pointing out of *when to use a capital letter, period, and a ques-*

tion mark. Before long, they will come in quickly, settle down, and look forward to the "Joke Riddle of the Day."

HUMOROUS QUOTES

Here are some *famous people* with quotes that might you *groan* . . . or laugh out loud?

"I looked up my family tree and found out I was the *sap*" ~ Rodney Dangerfield

"Between two evils, I always pick the one I *never* tried before." ~ Mae West

"When you are courting a nice girl an hour seems like a second. ~ When you sit on a red-hot cinder ~ a second seems like an hour. *That's relativity.*" ~ Albert Einstein

"It takes considerable knowledge just to realize the extent of your *own* ignorance." ~ Thomas Sowell

"A day without sunshine is like, you know, *night.*" ~ Steve Martin

"Tact is the ability to describe others as *they* see themselves." ~ Abraham Lincoln

"I love Mickey Mouse more than *any* woman I have ever known." ~ Walt Disney

"The *trouble* with having an open mind, of course, is that people will insist on coming along and trying to put things in it." ~ Terry Pratchett

"They say marriages are made in *Heaven*. But so is thunder and lightning." ~ Clint Eastwood

"Happiness is having a large, loving, caring, close-knit family in *another* city." ~ George Burns

"Prejudice is a great time saver. You can form opinions *without* having to get the facts." ~ E. B. White

"*Smoking kills.* If you're killed, you've lost a very important part of your life." ~ Brooke Shields

"It's simple, if it jiggles, it's *fat.*" ~ Arnold Schwarzenegger

"Any girl can be glamorous. All you have to do is stand still and look *stupid*." ~ Hedy Lamarr

"I'm like old wine. They don't bring me out very often—but I'm *well preserved*." ~ Rose Kennedy

"It all started when my dog began getting *free* roll over minutes." ~ Jay London

"I used to sell furniture for a living. The trouble was, it was my *own*." ~ Les Dawson

"I like long walks, especially when they are taken by people who *annoy* me." ~ Fred Allen

"I wanna make a jigsaw puzzle that's 40,000 pieces. And when you finish it, it says '*go outside*.'" ~ Demetri Martin

SHORT AND CUTE TEACHER/CHILD JOKES TO USE IN YOUR CLASSROOM.

So how are dogs and cats different?

1. Dogs will tilt their heads and try to understand *every word* you say. Cats will ignore you and *take a nap.*
2. When you come home from work, your dog will be happy and *lick your face.* Cats will still be *mad at you* for leaving in the first place.
3. Dogs will give you *unconditional love* until the day they die. Cats will *make you pay* for every mistake you've ever made, since the day you were born.
4. A dog knows when you're sad. And he'll try to *comfort you.* Cats don't care how you feel, as long as you remember where the *can opener* is.
5. Dogs will *bring you* your slippers. Cats will drop a *dead mouse* in your slippers.
6. When you take them for a ride, dogs will sit on the seat *next to you.* Cats have to have their *own private basket,* or they won't go at all.
7. Dogs *will come* when you call them. And they'll be happy. Cats will have someone take a message and *get back to you.*

8. Dogs will *play fetch* with you all day long. The only thing cats will play with all day long are *small rodents or bugs*, preferably ones that look like they're in pain.
9. Dogs will *wake you up* if the house is on fire. Cats will *quietly sneak* out the back door.

Submissons by: Albert *http://www.jokes4us.com/singleliners/topten reasonswhydogsarebetterpetsthancatsjoke.html*

To imagine children smiling and giggling over some of these jokes, makes one's heart sing. Some are even funny to adults, if you let them! *Remember your "inner child" is always there*, you just have to let it surface.

The following *website* is so much fun! It encourages reading and clever thinking for children: *https://www.jokesbykids.com/*

Let's now go to some of the funny stages of life . . . from a baby's perspective to end-of-life levity. If we can truly look at our beginning of living to the last stages humorously, we all would be better off.

THE MANY ROADS OF LIFE AND A FEW WORDS OF WISDOM

Great Truths that Little Children Have Learned

1. No matter how hard you try, you can't *baptize* cats.
2. When your Mom is mad at your Dad, *don't* let her brush your hair.
3. If your sister hits you, don't hit her back. They always "Catch" the *second* person.
4. Never ask your three-year-old brother to hold a *tomato*.
5. You *can't* trust dogs to watch your food.
6. Don't *sneeze* when someone is cutting your hair.
7. *Never* hold a Dust-Buster and a cat at the same time.
8. You can't hide a piece of *broccoli* in a glass of milk.
9. Don't wear polka-dot underwear under *white* shorts.
10. The best place to be when you're *sad* is Grandma's lap.

Great Truths That Adults Have Learned

1. Raising teenagers is like nailing Jell-O to a *tree*.
2. Wrinkles *don't* hurt.
3. Families are like fudge . . . mostly sweet, with a *few nuts*.
4. Today's mighty oak is just yesterday's nut that *held* its ground.
5. Laughing is good exercise. It's like jogging on the *inside*.
6. Middle age is when you choose your cereal for the fiber, *not* the toy.
7. Ever notice that anyone going slower than you is an *idiot*, but anyone going faster is a *maniac*?

Great Truth About Growing Old

1. Growing old is mandatory; growing up is *optional*.
2. Forget the health food. I need all the *preservatives* I can get.
3. When you fall down, you wonder what else you can do while you're *down* there.
4. You're getting old when you get the same sensation from a *rocking chair* that you once got from a roller coaster.
5. It's frustrating when you know all the answers, but *nobody* bothers to ask you the questions.
6. Time may be a great healer, but it's a *lousy* beautician.
7. Wisdom comes with age, but sometimes age comes *alone*.

The Four Stages of Life

1. You *believe* in Santa Claus.
2. You *don't* believe in Santa Claus.
3. You *are* Santa Claus.
4. You *look* like Santa Claus.

The Stages of Success

At age 4 success is . . . Not *piddling* in your pants.
At age 12 success is . . . Having friends.
At age 17 success is. . . Having a driver's license.

At age 35 success is . . . Having money.
At age 50 success is . . . Having money.
At age 70 success is . . . Having a driver's license.
At age 75 success is . . . Having friends.
At age 80 success is . . . Not *piddling* in your pants.

AND FINALLY

"Teachers are the only professionals who have to respond to bells every forty-five minutes and come out fighting." ~ Frank McCourt

"Knowledge is power, and enthusiasm pulls the switch." ~ Steve Droke

"It is more fun to talk with someone who doesn't use long, difficult words but rather short, easy words like *'What about lunch?'*" ~ A. A. Milne, *Pooh's Little Instruction Book*

"Millions saw the apple fall, but Newton was the one who asked why." ~ Bernard Mannes Baruch

"Once you get people laughing, they're listening." ~ Herbert Gardner

"Spoon feeding in the long run teaches us nothing but the shape of the spoon." ~ E. M. Forster

"I think you learn more if you're laughing at the same time." ~ Mary Ann Shaffer

"Summer: The time of the year when parents realize just how grossly underpaid teachers actually are." ~ Author Unknown

Always remember to *forget the troubles* that pass your way; but never *forget the blessings,* that come each day!

Have a wonderful day with many *smiles and giggles* AND WE ALL WILL LIVE LONGER! ~LINDA MARIE GILLIAM :)

BIBLIOGRAPHY

Allen, Steve. *"Dumbth": The Lost Art of Thinking, with 101 Ways to Reason Better and Improve Your Mind.* 2nd Edition. Buffalo, NY: Prometheus, 1998.

Amada, Gerald. "The Role of Humor in a College Mental Health Program." In *Advances in Humor and Psychotherapy*, edited by William F. Fry and Waleed A. Salameh, 157–182. Sarasota, FL: Professional Resource Press, 1993.

Backes, Anthony. "Aristophanes Would Laugh." *English Journal* 88.4 (1999): 34–42.

Baer, Teddi. "The Effect of Humor on Learning and Attitude for Adolescents when Incorporated into the Design of Computer Assisted Instruction." PhD diss., University of New Mexico, September, 1990.

Baumeister, Roy A., Joseph M. Boden, and Laura Smart. "Relationship of Threatened Egotism to Violence and Aggression: The Dark Side of High Self-Esteem." *Psychological Review* 103 (1996): 5–33.

Berk, Ronald A. "The Active Ingredients in Humor: Psychophysiological Benefits and Risks for Older Adults." *Educational Gerontology* 27 (2001): 323–339.

Berk, Ronald A. *Professors are from Mars, Students are from Snickers: How to Write and Deliver Humor in the Classroom and in Professional Presentations.* Virginia: Stylus, 2003.

Berk, Ronald A. *Humor as an Instructional Difibullator: Evidence-Based Techniques in Teaching and Assessments.* Virginia: Stylus, 2002.

Berk, Ronald A., and Joy P. Nanda. "Effects of Jocular Instructional Methods in Attitudes, Anxiety, and Achievement in Statistics Courses." *HUMOR: International Journal of Humor Research* 11.4 (1998): 383–410.

Boerman-Cornell, William. "The Five Humors." *English Journal* 88.4 (1999): 66–69.

Branden, Nathaniel. *How to Raise your Self-Esteem: The Proven Action-Oriented Approach to Greater Self-Respect and Self-Confidence.* New York: Bantam Books, 1988.

Branden, Nathaniel. *The Art of Living Consciously: The Power of Awareness to Transform Everyday Life.* New York: Fireside Books, 1999.

Branden, Nathaniel. *The Six Pillars of Self-Esteem: The Definitive Work on Self-Esteem by the Leading Pioneer in the Field.* New York: Bantam Books, 1995.

Briggs, Saga. "Intelligence & Humour: Are Smart People Funnier?" *InformEd*, February 21, 2015. https://www.opencolleges.edu.au/.../intelligence-humour-are-smart-people-funnier.

Brown, G. E., D. Brown, and J. Ramos. "Effects of a Laughing Versus a Non-Laughing Model on Humor: Responses in College Students." *Psychological Reports* 48.1 (1981): 35–40.

Bryant, Jennings, D. Brown, A. Silberberg, and S. Elliot. "Effects of Humorous Illustrations in College Textbooks." *Human Communication Research* 8 (1981): 43–57.

Bryant, Jennings, Paul Comisky, and Dolf Zillman. "The Relationship between College Teachers' Use of Humor in the Classroom and the Students' Evaluation of their Teachers." *Journal of Educational Psychology* 74 (1980): 511–519.

Bryant, Jennings, Jon S. Crane, Paul W. Comisky, and Dolf Zillmann. "Relationship between College Teachers' Use of Humor in the Classroom and Students' Evaluations of Their Teachers." *Journal of Educational Psychology* 72.4 (1980): 511–519.

Bryant, Jennings, J. Gula, and Dolf Zillman. "Humor in Communication Textbooks." *Communication Education* 29 (1980): 125–134.

Carlsen, Arne. "Only When I Laugh? Notes on the Becoming Interview." *Teachers and Teaching: Theory and Practice* 11.3 (2005): 239–255.

Carroll, James L. "Changes in Humor Appreciation of College Students in the Last Twenty-Five Years." *Psychological Reports* 65.3 (1989): 863–866.

Chesser, Lisa. "Comedy in the Classroom: 50 Ways to Bring Laughter into Any Lesson." Open Colleges, March 2013. https://www.opencolleges.edu.au/informed/features/comedy-in-the-classroom-50-ways-to-bring-laughter-into-any-lesson/.

Chopra, Deepak, MD. "Best Advice, Healthcare," Chopra Foundation, June 24, 2016. https://www.amazon.com/Perfect-Health-Complete-Revised-Updated/.../0609806947

Chopra, Deepak, MD, and Rudolph Tanzi, PhD. *"Super Genes," Quantum Healing* (Revised and Updated): *Exploring the Frontiers of Mind/Body Medicine.* New York: Bantam Books, 2015.

Civikly, Jean. "Humor and the Enjoyment of College Teaching." *New Directions for Teaching and Learning* 26 (1986): 61–70.

Clarke, Alastaire. *The Pattern Recognition Theory of Humor.* UK: Pyrrhic, 2008.

Cohen, Judith Beth. "Laughing in the Classroom: How Humor Enhances Education." *English Leadership Quarterly* 18.3 (1996): 2–4.

Cook, Guy. *Language Play, Language Learning.* New York, NY: Oxford University Press, 2000.

Cornett, Claudia E. *Learning through Laughter: Humor in the Classroom.* Bloomington, IN: Phi Delta Kappa Educational Foundation, 1986.

Coser, R. L. "Laughter among Colleagues." *Psychiatry* 23 (1960): 81–95.

Dalai Lama, Howard Cutler and Richard Davidson. *The Art of Happiness.* New York: Riverbend Books, 2009.

Davis, Jeff. "Speaking My Mind: On Humor." *English Journal* 88.4 (1999): 14–15.

Deer, Harriet, and Irving Deer. "Satire as Rhetorical Play." *Boundary 2* 5.3 (1977): 711–722.

Deneire, Marc. "Humor and Foreign Language Teaching." *HUMOR: International Journal of Humor Research* 8.3 (1995): 285–298.

Doucleef, Michaeleen. "The Sound of Laughter Tells More than You Think!" Daily Life Credit PNAS (proceedings of the Nat'l Academy of Sciences), 1-18, April 11, 2016. Accessed December 2016. http://www.npr.org/sections/goatsandsoda/2016/04/11/473414068/ha-ha-ha-haha-the-sound-of-laughter-tells-more-than-you-think.

Downs, Valerie C., Manoochehr Javadivi, and Jon F. Nussbaum. "An Analysis of Teachers' Verbal Communication within the Classroom: Use of Humor, Self-Disclosure, and Narratives." *Communication Education* 37.2 (1988), 127–141.

Droz, Marilyn, and Lori Ellis. *Laughing While Learning: Using Humor in the Classroom.* Longmont, CO: Sopris West, 1996.

Endlich, E. "Teaching the Psychology of Humor." *Teaching of Psychology* 20.3 (1993): 181–183.

Führ, Martin. "Coping Humor in Early Adolescence." *HUMOR: International Journal of Humor Research* 15.3 (2002): 283–304.

Führ, Martin. "Some Aspects on Form and Function of Humor in Early Adolescence." *HUMOR: International Journal of Humor Research* 14.1 (2001): 25–36.

Gallagher, Mary. "Teaching Comedy to Class Comedians." *English Journal* 71.2 (1982): 51–52.

Gerler, William R. *Educator's Treasury of Humor for All Occasions.* West Nyack, NY: Parker Publishing Co., 1972.

Gigliotti, E. "Let Me Entertain . . . er . . . Teach You: Gaining Attention through the Use of Slide Shows." *Journal of Continuing Education in Nursing* 26 (1995): 31–34.

Gilliam, Linda Marie. *The Seven Steps to Help Boys Love School: Teaching to their Passion for Less Frustration*. Maryland: Rowman & Littlefield, 2015.

Gladwell, Malcolm. *Outliers: The Story of Success*. New York: Little, Brown and Company, 2008.

Goleman, Daniel. "Emotional Intelligence." Accessed January 2017. https://www.learningtheories.com/emotional-intelligence-goleman.html.

Gorham, Joan, and Diane M. Christopher. "The Relationship of Teachers' Use of Humor in the Classroom to Immediacy and Student Learning." *Communication Education* 39.1 (1990): 46–62.

Harris, Sidney. *Can't You Guys Read? Cartoons on Academia*. New Brunswick, NJ: Rutgers University Press, 1991.

Harrison, N. "Using Humour as an Educational Technique." *Professional Nurse* 11 (1995): 198–199.

Hayes, Eleanor. "Science in School the Science of Humour: Allan Reiss." Accessed November 2016. http://www.scienceinschool.org/2010/issue17/allanreiss.

Hill, Deborah J. *Humor in the Classroom: A Handbook for Teachers (and Other Entertainers!)*. Springfield, IL: Charles C. Thomas, 1988.

Hill, Deborah J. *School Days, Fun Days: Creative Ways to Teach Humor Skills in the Classroom*. Springfield, IL: Charles C. Thomas, 1993.

Holmes, Janet, and Meredith Marra. "Over the Edge? Subversive Humor between Colleagues and Friends." *HUMOR: International Journal of Humor Research* 15.1 (2002): 65–88.

Johnson, H. A. "Humor as an Innovative Method for Teaching Sensitive Topics." *Educational Gerontology* 16.6 (1990): 547–559.

Johnson, Rob. *An ELT Notebook*. Accessed December 2016. http://eltnotebook.blogspot.com/2007/03/5-classroom-management-tips-to-silence.html.

Jones, Diane Carlson, Jodi Burrus Newman, and Shenna Bautista. "A Three-Factor Model of Teasing: The Influence of Friendship, Gender, and Topic on Expected Emotional Reactions to Teasing during Early Adolescence." *Social Development* 14.3 (2005): 421–439.

Kher, N., S. Molstad, and R. Donahue. "Using Humor in the College Classroom to Enhance Teaching Effectiveness in 'Dread Courses.'" *College Student Journal* 33 (1999): 400–406.

Kiernan, Henry, ed. "Humor and Laughter." A special issue of *English Leadership Quarterly* 18.3 (1996): 1–16.

King, J. "Laughter and Lesson Plans." *Techniques: Making Education and Career Connections* 74 (1999): 34–35.

Klein, Allen. *Teacherlaughs: Quips, Quotes, and Anecdotes about the Classroom from the Preschool to the College Lecture Hall*. New York, NY: Gramercy/Random House, 2006.

Korobkin, Debra. "Humor in the Classroom: Considerations and Strategies." *College Teaching* 36.4 (1988): 154–158.

Kuhrik, M., N. Kuhrik, and P. A. Berry. "Facilitating Learning with Humor." *Journal of Nursing Education* 36.7 (1997): 332–335.

Larson, Gary. "Humorous Teaching Makes Serious Learning." *Teaching English in the Two-Year College* 8.3 (1982): 197–199.

Liao, Chao-Chih. *Jokes, Humor and Good Teachers*. Chiayi, Taiwan: Crane Publishing Co., 2005.

Littleton, J. "Learning to Laugh, and Laughing to Learn." *Montessori Life* 10 (1998): 42–44.

Loomans, Diane, and Karen Kolberg. *The Laughing Classroom: Everyone's Guide to Teaching with Humor and Play*. Tiburon, CA: H. J. Kramer, 1993.

Lundgren, C. A., and P. R. Graves. "Funny Business: Should Humor Be Part of Teaching Business Education?" *Business Education Forum* 48.4 (1994): 11–13.

McGhee, Paul E. *How to Develop Your Sense of Humor: An 8-Step Humor Development Training Program*. Dubuque, IA: Kendall/Hunt, 1994.

McGhee, Paul E. *Humor and Children's Development: A Guide to Practical Applications*. New York, NY: Haworth, 1989.

McGhee, Paul E. *Humor Log for the 8-Step Humor Development Training Program*. Dubuque, IA: Kendall/Hunt, 1994.

McGhee, Paul E., Willibald Ruch, and Franz-Josef Hehl. "A Personality-Based Model of Humor Development during Adulthood." *Humor: International Journal of Humor Research* 3.2 (1990): 119–146.

McGhee, Paul E., PhD. "Laughter is Strong Medicine for Mind and Body." Accessed November 2016. https://womensconference.ce.byu.edu/sites/womensconference.ce.byu.edu/files/36c_0.pdf.

McGraw, Peter and Joel Warner. *The Humor Code: A Global Search for What Makes Things Funny*. New York: Simon & Schuster, 2014.

McMahon, Maureen. "Are We Having Fun Yet? Humor in the English Class." *English Journal* 88.4 (1999): 70–72.

McNeeley, Robert. NEA.org, "Using Humor in the Classroom: Laughter has the power to fuel engagement and help students learn." Accessed November 2016. http://www.nea.org/tools/52165.htm.

Marston, Ralph. "Commitment Matters." *The Daily Motivator*. August 3, 2015. http://greatday.com/motivate/150803.html.

Medgyes, P. "The Role of Humor in the Classroom." *Reflections on Language and Learning* (2001): 105–118.

Meeks, Lynn Langer. "Making English Classrooms Happier Places to Learn." *English Journal* 88.4 (1999): 73–81.

Miller, Geoffrey and Gil Greengross. "Humor Ability Reveals Intelligence, Predicts Mating Success, and Is Higher in Males." *Intelligence* 39 (2011): 188–192. Accessed December 2016. https://www.psychologytoday.com/sites/default/files/attachments/95822/humor-predicts-mating-success.pdf.

Morris, Barbra S. "Why Is George So Funny? Television Comedy, Trickster Heroism, and Cultural Studies." *English Journal* 88.4 (1999): 47–52.

Morrison, Mary Kay. *Using Humor to Maximize Learning: The Links between Positive Emotions and Education*. Maryland: Rowman & Littlefield, 2007.

Namka, Lynne. "Marvelhead," Tucson, AZ: Talk, Trust & Feel Therapeutics, 2003. Accessed January 2017. http://lynnenamka.com/anger-management.pdf.

Neuliep, James W. "An Examination of the Content of High School: Teacher's Humor in the Classroom and the Development of an Inductively Derived Taxonomy of Classroom Humor." *Communication Education* 40.4 (1991): 343–355.

Nilsen, Alleen Pace. "In Defense of Humor." *College English* 56.8 (1994): 928–933.

Nilsen, Alleen Pace. "Language for Fun: Humor in America." In *Living Language: Reading, Thinking and Writing*, 195–225. Boston, MA: Allyn and Bacon, 1999.

Nilsen, Alleen Pace. "Using Humor to Crack the Glass Ceiling." *Initiatives: Journal of the National Association for Women in Education* 56.2 (1994): 1–14.

Nilsen, Alleen Pace, and Don L. F. Nilsen. *Encyclopedia of 20th Century American Humor*. Westport, CT: Greenwood Press, 2000.

Nilsen, Alleen Pace, and Don L. F. Nilsen. "The Straw Man Meets His Match: Six Arguments for Studying Humor in English Classes." *English Journal* 88.4 (1999): 34–42.

Nilsen, Don L. F. "Humor and Creativity: Three Types—Ah, AHA, and HAHA!" *The Creative Child and Adult Quarterly* 15.4 (1990): 203–205.

Nilsen, Don L. F. "Humor, Maturity, and Education." *Humor Scholarship: A Research Bibliography*, 259–286. Westport, CT: Greenwood, 1993.

Nilsen, Don L. F. "Humor Studies Related to Composition, Rhetoric, and Discourse Theory." *English Leadership Quarterly* 18.3 (1996): 10–12.

Oaks, Dallin D. "Some Humor Software Matters: A Review of 'Mind Seducing Riddles.'" *English Leadership Quarterly* 18.3 (1996): 13.

Oppliger, Patrice A., and Dolf Zillman. "Disgust in Humor: Its Appeal to Adolescents." *HUMOR: International Journal of Humor Research* 10.4 (1997): 421–438.

Osteen, Joel. "Laugh a Little!" from *Today's Scripture* (Proverbs 17:22, NLT) 2015. https://kennardgroup.wordpress.com/2015/01/30/laugh-a-little-written-by-joel-osteen/

Parkin, C. J. "Humor, Health, and Higher Education: Laughing Matters." *Journal of Nursing Education* 28 (1989): 229–230.

Parrott, T. E. "Humor as a Teaching Strategy." *Nurse Educator* 19 (1994): 36–38.

Pellissier, Hank. "Your Second Grader's Brain," "Your Third Grader's Brain." *GreatSchools.* May 9, 2016. Accessed November 2016. http://www.greatschools.org/printview/parenting/behaviordiscipline/slideshows/4437-brain-second-grade.

Pollack, J. P., and P. D. Freda. "Humor, Learning, and Socialization in Middle Level Classrooms." *The Clearing House* 70 (1997): 176–178.

Powell, J. P., and L. W. Andresen. "Humour and Teaching in Higher Education." *Studies in Higher Education* 10.1 (1985): 74–90.

Priestly, J. B. "The Approach to Literature: Humor, Wit, Satire, Irony." *The English Journal* 18.7 (1929): 542–545.

Ransohoff, Rita. "Development Aspects of Humour and Laughter in Young Adolescent Girls." In *It's a Funny Thing, Humour,* Ed. Antony Chapman, 319–20. NY: Pergamon, 1977.

Ratey, John, MD. *Spark: The Revolutionary New Science of Exercise and the Brain.* New York: Little, Brown and Company, 2008.

Rhem, J. "Research Watch: Humor in the Classroom." *The National Teaching and Learning Forum* 7 (1998): 10–12.

Rastogi, Nina. "5 Leading Theories for Why We Laugh—and the Jokes That Prove Them Wrong." May, 2011. Accessed November 2016. http://www.slate.com/blogs/browbeat/2011/05/13/5_leading_theories_for_why_we_laugh_and_the_jokes_that_prove_them_wrong.html.

Robbins, J. "Using Humor to Enhance Learning in the Skills Laboratory." *Nurse Educator* 19 (1994): 39–41.

Robinson, Lawrence, Melinda Smith, MA, and Jeanne Segal, PhD. "Laughter is the Best Medicine: Health Benefits of Health and Laughter." Last modified June 1, 2014. Accessed January 2017. https://www.helpguide.org/articles/emotional-health/laughter-is-the-best-medicine.htm.

Ruggieri, Colleen A. "Laugh and Learn: Using Humor to Teach Tragedy." *English Journal* 88.4 (1999): 53–58.

Scheff, Thomas, and Sabina White. *Laughter and Stress: An Educational Programming Handbook for the College Community.* Santa Barbara, CA: Univ of Cal Laughter Project, 1984.

Schimel, John L. "Reflections on the Function of Humor in Psychotherapy, Especially with Adolescents." In *Advances in Humor and Psychotherapy,* Eds. William F. Fry and Waleed A. Salameh, 47–56. Sarasota, FL: Professional Resource Press, 1993.

Schmitz, John Robert. "Humor as a Pedagogical Tool in Foreign Language and Translation Courses." *HUMOR: International Journal of Humor Research* 15.1 (2002): 89–113.

Shannon, Donna M. "What Children Find Humorous in the Books They Read and How They Express their Responses." *HUMOR: International Journal of Humor Research* 12.2 (1999): 119–150.

Stopsky, Fred. "Humor: The Missing Ingredient to Successful Education." *English Leadership Quarterly* 18.3 (1996): 5–6.

Stuart, William D., and Lawrence B. Rosenfeld. "Student Perceptions of Teacher Humor and Classroom Climate." *Communication Research Reports* 11.1 (1994): 87–97.

Stutman, Michael, and Kevin Conklin. *The Ultimate Book of Inspiring Quotes for Kids.* Paperback—July 18, 2015. www.inspiremykids.com.

Tamblyn, Doni. *Laugh and Learn: 95 Ways to Use Humor for More Effective Teaching and Training.* NewYork, NY: AMACON (American Management Association), 2003.

Tatum, Tom. "Cruel and Unusual PUNishment (LOW Humor Is Better Than NO Humor)." *English Journal* 88.4 (1999): 62–65.

Taylor, Lynn. "Add Humor to Your Job and Boost Your Career." *Psychology Today.* April 13, 2015. Accessed December 2016. https://www.psychologytoday.com/blog/tame-your-terrible-office-tyrant.

Unland, M. K., and B. Kleiner. "How to Enhance Your Sense of Humor." *Agency Sales Magazine* 25 (1995): 56–61.

Viorist, Judith. *Alexander and the Terrible, Horrible, No Good, Very Bad Day*. Illus by Ray Cruz. New York: Atheneum, 1972.

Wandersee, J. H. "Humor as a Teaching Strategy." *The American Biology Teacher* 44.4 (1982): 212–218.

Watson, M. J., and S. Emerson. "Facilitate Learning with Humor." *Journal of Nursing Education* 27 (1988): 89–90.

Wanzer, Frymier, Melissa Bekelja Wanzer, and Ann Bainbridge Frymier. "The Relationship Between Student Perceptions of Instructor Humor and Students' Reports of Learning" *Communication Education* 48.1 (1999): 48–62.

Wechsler, Robert, ed. *Humor for Grownups*. North Haven, CT: Catbird Press, 1999.

Welker, William A. "Humor in Education: A Foundation for Wholesome Living." *College Student Journal* 11 (1977): 252–54.

White, L. A., and D. J. Lewis. "Humor: A Teaching Strategy to Promote Learning." *Journal of Nursing Staff Development* 6 (1990): 60–64.

Wolfelt MD, Alan. Director of the Center for Loss and Life Transition in Fort Collins, Colorado. Accessed January 2017. https://www.centerforloss.com.

Zajdman, Anat. "Humorous Events in the Classroom: The Teachers' Perspective." *Journal of Research and Development in Education* 26.2 (1993): 106–115.

Zajdman, Anat. "Humorous FTAs—Humor as Strategy." *Journal of Pragmatics* 23 (1995): 325–339.

Zillman, Dolf, and Jennings Bryant. "Uses and Effects of Humor in Educational Ventures." In *Handbook of Humor Research*, Eds. Paul E. McGee and Jeffrey H. Goldstein, 173–193. New York, NY: Springer-Verlag, 1983.

Ziv, Avner. "The Influence of Humorous Atmosphere on Divergent Thinking." *Contemporary Educational Psychology* 8 (1983): 68–75.

Ziv, Avner. "Teaching and Learning with Humor: Experiment and Replication." *Journal of Experimental Education* 57 (1988): 5–15.